STYLE AND IDEA

STYLE and IDEA

by
ARNOLD SCHOENBERG

PHILOSOPHICAL LIBRARY
New York

Printed in the United States of America

Editor's Foreword

ARNOLD SCHOENBERG, as an author, has his own personality and ideas, not only in German but also in English. Several of the essays now composing *Style and Idea* were originally written in German. In translating these, I have, at the author's wish, adhered as literally to the original style as English usage allows. Thus there should be a certain consistency of expression between these and the later essays which were written in English but which still bear the earmarks of Schoenberg's individual German style.

Schoenberg himself has elucidated his attitude towards his own manner of writing in English as follows:

". . . I do not plan to hide the fact that I am not born in this language and I do not want to parade adorned by stylistic merits of another person." Obedience to this viewpoint has governed editorial activities throughout.

It may also be stated that, of set purpose, no attempt has been made to eliminate any possible inconsistencies in the points of view expressed in the different essays. It should be remembered that they represent the product of nearly forty years of Schoenberg's intellectual activity, and hence reflect the growth and development of his ideas during that time. What they do not present is a fixed dogma and no such thing should be sought for in them.

DIKA NEWLIN

Table of Contents

The Relationship to the Text[1]

THERE ARE relatively few people who are capable of understanding, purely in terms of music, what music has to say.
The assumption that a piece of music must summon up images of one sort or another, and that if these are absent the
piece of music has not been understood or is worthless, is as
widespread as only the false and banal can be. Nobody expects such a thing from any other art, but rather contents
himself with the effects of its material, although in the other
arts the material-subject, the represented object, automatically
presents itself to the limited power of comprehension of the
intellectually mediocre. Since music as such lacks a material-
subject, some look beyond its effects for purely formal beauty, others for poetic procedures. Even Schopenhauer, who at
first says something really exhaustive about the essence of
music in his wonderful thought, "The composer reveals the
inmost essence of the world and utters the most profound
wisdom in a language which his reason does not understand,
just as a magnetic somnambulist gives disclosures about things
which she has no idea of when awake"—even he loses himself later when he tries to translate details of this language
which the reason does not understand into our terms. It must,
however, be clear to him that in this translation into the
terms of human language, which is abstraction, reduction to
the recognizable, the essential, the language of the world,
which ought perhaps to remain incomprehensible and only
perceptible, is lost. But even so he is justified in this procedure, since after all it is his aim as a philosopher to represent
the essence of the world, its unsurveyable wealth, in terms of
concepts whose poverty is all too easily seen through. And

---

1 *Der Blaue Reiter*, 1912.

[1]

Wagner too, when he wanted to give the average man an indirect notion of what he as a musician had looked upon directly, did right to attach programs to Beethoven's symphonies.

Such a procedure becomes disastrous when it becomes general usage. Then its meaning becomes perverted to the opposite; one tries to recognize events and feelings in music as if they *must* be there. On the contrary, in the case of Wagner it is as follows: the impression of the "essence of the world" received through music becomes productive in him and stimulates him to a poetic transformation in the material of another art. But the events and feelings which appear in this transformation were not contained in the music, but are merely the material which the poet uses only because so direct, unpolluted and pure a mode of expression is denied to poetry, an art still bound to subject-matter.

The capacity of pure perception is extremely rare and only to be met with in men of high calibre. This explains why professional arbiters become embarrassed by certain difficulties. That our scores become harder and harder to read, that the relatively few performances pass by so quickly, that often even the most sensitive, purest man can receive only fleeting impressions—all this makes it impossible for the critic, who must report and judge, but who is usually incapable of imagining alive a musical score, to do his duty even with that degree of honesty upon which he might perhaps decide if it would do him no harm. Absolutely helpless he stands in the face of purely musical effect, and therefore he prefers to write about music which is somehow connected with a text: about program music, songs, operas, etc. One could almost excuse him for it when one observes that operatic conductors, from whom one would like to find out something about the music of a new opera, prattle almost exclusively about the libretto, the theatrical effectiveness, and the performers. Indeed, since musicians have acquired culture and think they have to demonstrate this by avoiding shop-talk, there are scarcely any musicians with whom one can talk about music. But Wagner, whom they like so much to cite as an example, wrote a tremendous amount about purely musical matters; and I am sure that he would unconditionally repudiate these consequences of his misunderstood efforts.

Therefore, it is nothing but a comfortable way out of this dilemma when a music critic writes of an author that his composition does not do justice to the words of the poet. The "scope of this newspaper," which is always most limited in space just when necessary evidence should be brought in, is always most willing to help out the lack of ideas, and the artist is really pronounced guilty because of "lack of evidence." But the evidence for such assertions, when it is once brought out, is rather evidence for the contrary, since it merely shows how somebody would make music who does not know how to—how accordingly music ought in no case to look if it has been composed by an artist. This is even true in the case of a composer's writing criticisms. Even if he is a good composer. For in the moment when he writes criticisms he is not a composer, not *musically inspired*. If he were inspired he would not describe how the piece ought to be composed, but would compose it himself. This is quicker and even easier for one who can do it, and is more convincing.

In reality, such judgments come from the most banal notion possible, from a conventional scheme according to which a certain dynamic level and speed in the music must correspond to certain occurrences in the poem and must run exactly parallel to them. Quite aside from the fact that *this* parallelism, or one even more profound, can also be present when externally the opposite seems to be presented—that, for example, a tender thought can be expressed by a quick and violent theme because the following violence will develop from it more organically—quite aside from this, such a scheme is already to be rejected because it is conventional; because it would lead to making music into a language which "composes and thinks" for every man. And its use by critics leads to manifestations like an article which I once read somewhere, "Faults of Declamation in Wagner," in which someone showed how he would have composed certain passages if Wagner had not beaten him to it.

A few years ago I was deeply ashamed when I discovered in several Schubert songs, well-known to me, that I had absolutely no idea what was going on in the poems on which they were based. But when I had read the poems it became clear to me that I had gained absolutely nothing for the understanding of the songs thereby, since the poems did not make it necessary for me to change my conception of the musical interpretation in the slightest degree. On the contrary, it appeared that, without knowing the poem, I had grasped the content, the real content, perhaps even more profoundly than if I had clung to the surface of the mere thoughts expressed in words. For me, even more decisive than this experience was the fact that, inspired by the sound of the first words of the text, I had composed many of my songs straight through to the end without troubling myself in the slightest about the continuation of the poetic events, without even grasping them in the ecstasy of composing, and that only days later I thought of looking back to see just what was the real poetic content of my song. It then turned out, to my greatest astonishment, that I had never done greater justice to the poet than when, guided by my first direct contact with the sound of the beginning, I divined everything that obviosuly had to follow this first sound with inevitability.

Thence it became clear to me that the work of art is like every other complete organism. It is so homogeneous in its composition that in every little detail it reveals its truest, inmost essence. When one cuts into any part of the human body, the same thing always comes out—blood. When one hears a verse of a poem, a measure of a composition, one is in a position to comprehend the whole. Even so, a word, a glance, a gesture, the gait, even the color of the hair, are sufficient to reveal the personality of a human being. So I had completely understood the Schubert songs, together with their poems, from the music alone, and the poems of Stefan George from their sound alone, with a perfection that by analysis and synthesis could hardly have been attained, but certainly not surpassed. However, such impressions usually address themselves to the intellect later on, and demand that it prepare them for general applicability, that it dissect and sort them, that it measure and test them, and resolve into details what we possess as a whole. And even artistic creation often goes this roundabout way before it arrives at the real conception. When Karl Kraus calls language the mother of thought, and Wassily Kandinsky and Oskar Kokoschka paint pictures the objective theme of which is hardly more than an excuse to improvise in colors and forms and to express themselves as only the musician expressed himself until now, these are symptoms of a gradually expanding knowledge of the true nature of art. And with great joy I read Kandinsky's book *On the Spiritual in Art,* in which the road for painting is pointed out and the hope is aroused that those who ask about the text, about the subject-matter, will soon ask no more.

Then there will become clear what was already made clear in another instance. No one doubts that a poet who works with historical material may move with the greatest freedom, and that a painter, if he still wanted to paint historical pictures today, would not have to compete with a history professor. One has to hold to what a work of art intends to offer, and not to what is merely its intrinsic cause. Furthermore, in all music composed to poetry, the exactitude of the reproduction of the events is as irrelevant to the artistic value as is the resemblance of a portrait to its model; after all, no one can check on this resemblance any longer after a hundred years, while the artistic effect still remains. And it does not remain because, as the Impressionists perhaps believe, a real man (that is, the one who is apparently represented) speaks to us, but because the artist does so—he who has expressed himself here, he whom the portrait must resemble in a higher reality. When one has perceived this, it is also easy to understand that the outward correspondence between music and text, as exhibited in declamation, tempo and dynamics, has but little to do with the inward correspondence, and belongs to the same stage of primitive imitation of nature as the copying of a model. Apparent superficial divergences can be necessary because of parallelism on a higher level. Therefore, the judgment on the basis of the text is just as reliable as the judgment of albumen according to the characteristics of carbon.

Gustav Mahler

INSTEAD OF USING many words, perhaps I should do best simply to say: I believe firmly and steadfastly that Gustav Mahler was one of the greatest men and artists. For there are only two possibilities of convincing someone of an artist's greatness: the first and better way is to perform his work; the second, which I am forced to use, is to transmit my belief in this work to others.

Man is petty! Truly, we should have faith that our belief will transmit itself directly. Our passion for the object of our veneration must so inflame us that everyone who comes near us must burn with us, must be consumed by the same ardor and worship the same fire which is also sacred to us. This fire should burn so brightly in us that we become transparent, so that its light shines forth and illuminates even the one who, until now, walked in darkness. An apostle who does not glow preaches heresy. He to whom the halo of sanctity is denied does not carry the image of a god within himself. For the apostle does not shine by himself, but by a light which uses his body merely as a shell; the light pierces the shell, but it graciously grants the glowing one the appearance of shining by himself. We, who are inspired, must have faith; men will sympathize with this ardor, men will see our light shining. Men will honor the one whom we worship—even without our doing anything about it.

Man is petty. We do not believe enough in the whole thing, in the great thing, but demand irrefutable details. We depend too little upon that capacity which gives us an impression of the object as a totality containing within itself all details in their corresponding relationships. We believe that we understand what is natural; but the miracle is extremely natural, and the natural is extremely miraculous.

[7]

The more exactly we observe, the more enigmatic does the simplest matter become to us. We analyze because we are not satisfied with comprehending nature, effect and function of a totality as a totality and, when we are not able to put together again exactly what we have taken apart, we begin to do injustice to that capacity which gave us the whole together with its spirit, and we lose faith in our finest ability—the ability to receive a total impression.

I shall give an example which will seem familiar to anyone who observes himself carefully enough. I remember distinctly that the first time I heard Mahler's Second Symphony I was seized, especially in certain passages, with an excitement which expressed itself even physically, in the violent throbbing of my heart. Nevertheless, when I left the concert I did not fail to test what I had heard according to those requirements which were known to me as a musician, and with which, as is generally believed, a work of art must unconditionally comply. Thus I forgot the most important circumstance—that the work had, after all, made an unheard-of impression on me, inasmuch as it had enchanted me into an involuntary sympathy. Indeed, a work of art can produce no greater effect than when it transmits the emotions which raged in the creator to the listener, in such a way that they also rage and storm in him. And I was overwhelmed; completely overwhelmed.

The intellect is skeptical; it does not trust the sensual, and it trusts the supersensual even less. If one is overwhelmed, the intellect maintains that there are many means which might bring forth such an overwhelming emotion. It reminds us that no one can view a tragic event in life without being most deeply moved; it reminds us of the melodramatic horror-play, whose effect none can escape; it reminds us that there are higher and lower means, artistic and inartistic. It tells us that realistic, violent incidents—as, for example, the torture scene in *Tosca*—which are unfailingly effective should not be used by an artist, because they are too cheap, too accessible to everyone. And it forgets that such realistic means will never be employed in music, and especially not in the symphony, because music is always unreal. In music, no one is ever really killed or tortured unjustly; here, there is never any event which could awaken sympathy *in itself*, for only musical matters appear. And only when these events have power to speak for themselves—only when this alternation of high and low tones, fast and slow rhythms, loud and soft sounds, tells of the most unreal things that exist—only then are we moved to utmost sympathy. He who has once felt the impact of this purity remains immune to all other impressions! It is entirely out of the question that musical sentiment can be traced to impure sources, for the means of music are unreal, and only reality is impure!

A man who has been overwhelmed and knows that his artistic and ethical culture is on a high level, and thus has confidence in himself and believes in his culture, need not concern himself with the question of whether the means were artistic. And he who is not overwhelmed is concerned even less. It is enough for him that he was neither overwhelmed—nor repelled! Why, then all the bombastic words? For this reason: we like to make our judgments agree with those of others at any price, and when this does not work, we strive to achieve the advantage of a well-founded and well-fortified position of our own. Differences of understanding are only partly causes of splitting into parties; far more is due to the justifications. They make the disagreement endless. It is not certain that what I call red is really the same in the eye of another as it is in mine. And nevertheless agreement is easily reached here, so that there is no doubt about what is red and what is green. But the moment one tried to explain *why* this is red, that green, dissension would certainly set in. The simple experience of the senses: "I see what is called red" or "I feel that I am overwhelmed" can be easily stated by anyone who is intelligent enough. And he should have the courage to consider the fact that he is not overwhelmed as something self-evident but completely unimportant to the object, just as one who is deaf may not disown sounds, or one who is color-blind, colors.

The work of art exists even if no one is overwhelmed by it, and the attempt to rationalize one's feelings about it is superfluous, because this attempt always exhibits the characteristics of the subject and never those of the object: the onlooker is color-blind, the listener deaf; the art-lover was in the wrong mood, was unfitted (perhaps only at the moment, perhaps permanently) to receive an artistic impression.

But how does it come about that someone who has tried with the best will in the world to understand arrives at such perverted judgments, in spite of having received an impression? Here and there one has come across a passage which one does not like; a melody which one finds banal, which seems to be unoriginal; a continuation which one does not understand, for which one thinks to find a better substitute; a voice-leading which seems to scorn all the requirements heretofore set up for good voice-leading. One is a musician, belongs to the guild, is capable of doing something oneself (or perhaps not!) and always knows exactly how the thing should be done, if indeed it should be done at all. It is pardonable that such a one feels justified in cavilling at details. For we all cavil over the works of the greatest masters. There is scarcely anyone who, if he received an order to create the world better than the Lord God Almighty had done it, would not undertake the task without further ado. Everything which we do not understand we take for an error; everything which makes us uncomfortable we take for a mistake of its creator. And we do not stop to think that, since we do not understand the meaning, silence, respectful silence, would be the only fitting response. And admiration, boundless admiration.

But, as has been said, we are petty; simply because we cannot survey the great thing in its entirety, we concern ourselves with its details—and, as punishment for our presumptuous behavior, we fail even there. We are wrong all the way down the line. In every case where human understanding tries to abstract from divine works the laws according to which they are constructed, it turns out that we find only laws which characterize our cognition through thinking and our power of imagination. We are moving in a circle. We always see and recognize only ourselves, only, at most, our own being, as often as we think we are describing the essence of a thing outside ourselves. And these laws, which are, at best, those of our intellectual capacity, we apply as a yardstick to the work of the creator! On the basis of such laws, we judge the work of the great artist!

Perhaps it has never been harder to give an artist his proper due than today. Overvaluation and undervaluation have probably hardly ever before been such inevitable results of the business of art. And it has never been more difficult for the public to tell who is really great and who is just a big name of the day. Countless men are producing. They cannot all be geniuses. A few set the pace, the others merely imitate. But if the many imitators want to stay in the race, they must quickly find out what is the latest brand good in the market. The publishers, the press and publicity take care of this, and achieve the result that one who is creating something new is not left alone for long. Bee-like industry, which today in all fields achieves the success which only talent should have, asserts itself here too, and brings it about that the epoch is expressed not by the solitary great man, but by a throng of little men. The truly great have always had to flee from the present into the future, but the present has never belonged so completely to the mediocre as it does today. And no matter how great the gap, they will try to bridge it— they even stake out their claims on the future. No one wants to write just for today, even if he can hardly be believed in for as long as one day. There are only geniuses, and to them belongs even the future. How can we find the right way here? How can we tell who is really great, when the high average is so widely distributed that we forget height in favor of breadth? We really talk far too much about the Alps and too little about Mont Blanc.

It is almost excusable that the public fails here, for there are always many who provide what is suitable to the needs of our time in a much more accessible form than can be offered by someone who already belongs to the future. One can be modern today without aiming for the best. One has so wide a selection among the moderns that the spirit of the time is accessible "to the most refined taste and also to the less well-to-do, in all shades and in all price-brackets." Who will strain himself under these circumstances? One is modern —that is enough. Eventually, one is even ultramodern—that makes one interesting. One has a program, principles, taste. One knows what it is all about. One knows all the critical clichés. One knows exactly what are the current trends in art. Yes, one could almost establish in advance the very problems and methods with which the art of the immediate future will have to concern itself, and I am only surprised that no one has yet hit upon the idea of combining all these possibilities and concocting a guide-book to the future.

This is the unexpected result which Wagner attained when he created Beckmesser as a warning for too-hasty critics. Everyone considers himself a connoisseur of new art, and the Beckmessers of today affirm that they have become more "broad-minded." But this is obviously false, for the good is and remains good and must therefore be persecuted, and the bad is and remains bad and must therefore be promoted. Thus the praised broadening of the mind appears to be rather softening of the brain. For these men have lost every standpoint and all limitations, since they do not notice that they are even more narrow-minded than those who at least praised what "ran according to their rules."

Otherwise, the same old catchwords could not always be dragged in every time that a really great man was under consideration. For example: Mahler has written unusually extensive works. Everyone feels, or thinks he knows, that in them something exceptionally high and great strives for expression. What worn-out commonplace would come more readily to a broad-minded man than this: he strives for the highest but does not possess the strength to perform what he desires? And who says it? Those critics who have accommodated their very broad-mindedness to the common interest. Those who are less good, as well as the very bad ones—for it is a point of honor with them to agree on basic things. This sentence is, therefore, one of those thoughtless clichés which must be hated above all because they are almost without exception applied to those men to whom they are least appropriate. Little men come out of it very well. But as soon as it is said of someone that he strives for the highest, etc., I know at once that he has either not striven for it or has not reached it! That is, after all, something to be depended upon. By which measurement is that greatness established for which Mahler is supposed to have striven in vain? In the dimensions of the works, and in a circumstance which seems to me immaterial in relation to the real aspirations of the artist: in the subject-matter and texts on which several movements of his symphonies are based. Mahler has spoken of death, of resurrection, of fate; he has composed *Faust*. And these are supposed to be the greatest things. But nearly every musician in earlier times composed church music and concerned himself with God—that is, with something still higher; and he could strive unconcernedly for the highest, without anyone's measuring his work with that yardstick. On the contrary, if it is really great to stand in the shadow of the greatest themes, one ought actually to require this of an artist. In reality, there is only one greatest goal towards which the artist strives: *to express himself*. If that succeeds, then the artist has achieved the greatest possible success; next to that, everything else is unimportant, for everything else is included in it: death, resurrection, Faust, fate—but also the lesser and yet not less important moments, the emotions of the soul and spirit which make a man creative. Mahler, too, tried only to express himself. And that he succeeded can be doubted by no one who is in the slightest degree capable of comprehending how isolated this music has remained, although the imitators are so busy trying to catch up with everything that has a chance of capturing the market. That there are no imitations of these symphonies which resemble their model in the slightest degree, that this music seems inimitable (like everything that one man alone can achieve)— all this proves that Mahler was capable of the greatest possible achievement of an artist: self-expression! He expressed only himself, and not death, fate and Faust. For that could also be composed by others. He expressed only that which, independent of style and flourish, portrays himself and himself alone, and which therefore would remain inaccessible to anyone else who tried to achieve it merely by imitating the style. But this style itself seems, in an enigmatic and heretofore unfamiliar way, to exclude imitation. Perhaps this is because here, for the first time, a mode of expression is so inseparably bound up with the subject to which it applies that what usually appears merely as a symptom of the outward form is here, simultaneously, material and construction as well.

I wish to concern myself with several things which were said against Mahler's work. Next come two accusations: against his sentimentality and against the banality of his themes. Mahler suffered much from these accusations. Against the latter, one is almost defenseless; against the former, completely so. Think of it: an artist, in all good faith, writes down a theme just as his need for expression and his feelings dictate it to him, without changing a note. If he wanted to escape banality, it would be easy for him. The meanest tunesmith, who looks harder at his notes than into himself, is capable of "making" a banal theme interesting with a few strokes of his pen. And most interesting themes originate in this way—just as every painter can avoid trashy detailed painting by painting just as trashily with broad strokes. And now imagine this: this most sensitive, spiritually most elevated man, from whom we have heard the most profound words—pre-

[14]

cisely this man was supposed to be unable to write unbanal themes, or at least to alter them until they no longer appeared banal!

I think he simply did not notice it, and for one reason alone: *his themes are actually not banal.*

Here I must confess that I, too, at first considered Mahler's themes banal. I consider it important to admit that I was Saul before I became Paul, since it may thence be deduced that those "fine discriminations" of which certain opponents are so proud were not foreign to me. *But they are foreign to me now,* ever since my increasingly intense perception of the beauty and magnificence of Mahler's work has brought me to the point of admitting that it is not fine discrimination, but, on the contrary, the most blatant lack of the power of discrimination, which produces such judgments. I had found Mahler's themes banal, although the whole work had always made a profound impression on me. Today, with the worst will in the world, I could not react this way. Consider this: if they were really banal I should find them far more banal today than formerly. For banal means rustic, and describes something which belongs to a low grade of culture, to no culture at all. In lower grades of culture there is found, not what is absolutely false or bad, but what used to be right, what is obsolete, what has been outlived, what is no longer true. The peasant does not behave badly, but archaically, just as those of higher rank behaved before they knew better. Therefore, the banal represents a backward state of ethics and state of mind, which was once the state of mind of the higher ranks; it was not banal from the beginning, but became banal only when it was pushed aside by new and better customs. But it cannot rise up again—once it is banal, it must stay banal. And if I now maintain that I can no longer find these themes banal, they can never have been so; for a banal idea, an idea which appears obsolete and worn-out to me, can only appear more banal on closer acquaintance—but in no case noble. But if now I discover that the oftener I look at these ideas the more new beauties and noble traits are added to them, doubt is no longer possible: the idea is the opposite of banal. It is not something which we were long ago done with and cannot misunderstand, but something the deepest meaning of which is as yet far from completely revealed, something so profound that we have not become aware of more than its superficial appearance. And, in fact, this has happened not only to Mahler, but also to nearly all other great composers, who had to submit to the accusation of banality. I call to mind only Wagner and Brahms. I think that the change in my feeling provides a better yardstick than the judgment on first hearing which everyone is very quick to come out with as soon as he runs into a situation which he really does not understand.

The artist is even more defenseless against the accusation of sentimentality than against that of banality. Mahler, halfway giving in to the latter because his self-confidence had been undermined, could defend himself by saying that one ought not to look at the theme, but at what comes out of it. He need not have done this. But the criticism was so general that he was forced to believe himself in the wrong—after all, the best musicians and all the other worst people were saying so! But there is no defense against the other accusation, that of sentimentality. That hits home as hard as calling something trash. Everyone who really likes nothing but trash is in a position to give a stab in the back to the most honorable and important man, to the one who turns most violently away from the merely pleasing (which after all, is really what trash amounts to), and thus to degrade him and also to rob him of inner security. The way of attacking significant works of art is different now from what it used to be. Formerly, an artist was reproached if he did not know enough; now it is a cause for criticism if he knows too much. Smoothness, which was formerly a quality to be sought, is today an error, for it is trashy. Yes, one paints with broad strokes today! Everyone paints with broad strokes, and he who does not paint with broad strokes is trashy. And he who does not possess humor or superficiality, heroic greatness and Greek serenity, is sentimental. It is very fortunate that the ethics of Red Indian stories have not yet become the model for our attitudes towards art. Otherwise, estheticians would consider only Indian lack of sensitivity to pain, in addition to Greek serenity, as unsentimental.

What is true feeling? But that is a question of feeling! That can only be answered by feeling! Whose feelings are right? Those of the man who disputes the true feelings of another, or those of the man who gladly grants another his true feelings, so long as he says just what he has to say? Schopenhauer explains the difference between sentimentality and true sorrow. He chooses as an example Petrarch, whom the painters of broad strokes would surely call sentimental, and shows that the difference consists in this: true sorrow elevates itself to resignation, while sentimentality is incapable of that, but always grieves and mourns, so that one has finally lost "earth and heaven together." To elevate oneself to resign-ation: how can one speak of a sentimental theme, when this complaining, sorrowing theme may, in the course of events, elevate itself to resignation? That is as wrong as when one speaks of a "witty phrase." The whole man is witty—full of wit—but not the single phrase. The whole work can be senti-mental, but not the single passage. For its relationship to the whole is decisive: what it becomes, what importance it is granted in the whole. And how Mahler's music elevates it-self to resignation! Are "heaven and earth together" lost here, or is there not rather portrayed here, for the first time, an earth on which life is worth living, and is there not then praised a heaven which is more than worth living for? Think of the Sixth Symphony—of the frightful struggle in the first movement. But then, its sorrow-torn upheaval automatically generates its opposite, the unearthly passage with the cowbells, whose cool, icy comfort is bestowed from a height which is reached only by one who soars to resignation; only he can hear it who understands what heavenly voices whisper without animal warmth.

Then, the Andante movement. How pure is its tone to one who knows today that it was not banality which kept it from pleasing, but the strangeness of the emotions of a thoroughly unusual personality which kept it from being understood! Or the post-horn solo in the Third Symphony, at first with the divided high violins, then, even more beautiful if possible, with the horns. This is a mood of nature, of "Greek serenity," if it must be so—or, more simply, of the most marvelous beauty, for one who does not need such slogans! Or the last movement of the Third! The entire Fourth, but especially its fourth movement! And its third! And its second and first movements too! Yes, all of them! Naturally, all of them; for there are no beautiful passages by great masters, but only entire beautiful works.

Incredibly irresponsible is another accusation made against Mahler: that his themes are unoriginal. In the first place, art does not depend upon the single component part alone; therefore, music does not depend upon the theme. For the work of art, like every living thing, is conceived as a whole—just like a child, whose arm or leg is not conceived separately. The inspiration is not the theme, but the whole work. And it is not the one who writes a good theme who is inventive, but the one to whom a whole symphony occurs at once. But in the second place, these themes are original. Naturally, he who looks at only the first four notes will find reminiscences. But he behaves as foolishly as one who looks for original words in an original poem; for the theme consists not of a few notes, but of the musical destinies of these notes. The small form which we call a theme ought never to be the only yardstick for the large form, of which it is relatively the smallest component part. But the observation of nothing but the smallest parts of the theme must lead to those abuses against which Schopenhauer turned when he demanded that one must use the most ordinary words to say the most extraordinary things.

And this must also be possible in music; with the most ordinary successions of tones one ought to be able to say the most extraordinary things. Mahler does not need that as an excuse. Although he strove for the most far-reaching simplicity and naturalness, his themes have a structure all their own—true, not in the sense in which many writers play around with words. For an example, I wish to cite one writer who always left out the reflexive pronoun in order to achieve a personal note. But Mahler's themes are original in the highest sense, when one observes with what fantasy and art, with what wealth of variation there comes out of a few such tones an endless melody, which is often difficult to analyze even for someone skilled in that process—when one takes note of the thoroughly original musical phenomena arrived at by each of his themes in the most natural way possible. From the fact that this way is so completely original one can recognize which elements are to be ascribed to the brain and which to the heart. That is: the way, the goal, the whole development of everything at once, the whole movement; naturally, the theme as well—but not the first few relatively unimportant notes!

One must go even further: it is not at all necessary for a piece of music to have an original theme. Otherwise, Bach's chorale preludes would not be works of art. But they certainly are works of art!

So it always goes with very great men. At each are fired all those accusations of which the opposite is true. Yes, *all,* and with such accuracy that one must be taken aback by it. For this shows, contrary to one's expectations, that the qualities of an author are really noticed already at the first hearing, but are merely wrongly interpreted. Whenever the most personal of the composer's peculiarities appear, the listener is struck. But instead of recognizing immediately that this is a special feature, he interprets the blow as a blow of offense. He believes that there is a mistake, a fault here, and fails to see that it is a merit.

[19]

One should really have been able to recognize Mahler's high artistry on one's first glance at his scores. Today I cannot understand at all how this escaped me. The unheard-of simplicity, clarity, and beauty of arrangement immediately struck me in these scores. It remined me of the aspect of the greatest masterworks. But I did not yet know then what I know today: that it is entirely out of the question for someone to accomplish something masterly in any respect who is not a master in every respect. Therefore, anyone who can write such scores has one of those minds in which perfection automatically originates. And the concept of perfection completely excludes the concept of imperfection; therefore, it is not possible to give a representation of an imperfect thing which produces the impression of perfection. From the aspect of the score alone a musician who has a feeling for form must recognize that this music can only be by a master.

And Gustav Mahler had to endure being told that he knew nothing. As a matter of fact, opinion was divided. Some asserted that he could do everything in a very refined manner, and, in particular, orchestrated very effectively, but that he had no inventiveness and that his music was empty. These were the more complicated blockheads. The simpler ones were good at part-leading, and therefore scorned instrumentation and everything else which could be accomplished by another and not by them. They knew very well that one ought not to compose in this manner. These are the same people who have always known how masters ought not to compose, if they want to remain such bunglers as these amateurs. They have always set up the standards for Beethoven, Wagner, Hugo Wolf, and Bruckner, and in every period would have known exactly what the only right thing is. Nothing has survived of this omniscience but its ridicule— but that permeates the entire history of music.

The artistry of melodic construction is especially striking in Mahler, who wrote entirely tonally, and to whom, therefore, many harmonic means of contrast were not as yet avail-

able for his purposes. It is incredible how long these melodies
can become, although certain chords have to be repeated in
the process. And in spite of this no monotony sets in. On
the contrary, the longer the theme lasts, the greater is its
final impetus; the force which drives its development increases with uniformly accelerating motion. No matter how
hot the theme may have been *in statu nascendi,* after a while
it is not burnt out, but burns even brighter, and whereas in
someone else's music it would long since have exhausted itself
and vanished, here it only now rises to the highest pitch
of excitement. If that is not capability, it is at least potency.
Something similar appears in the first movement of the
Eighth Symphony. How often does this movement come to
E flat, for instance on a four-six chord! I would cut that out
in any student's work, and advise him to seek out another
tonality. And, incredibly, here it is right! Here it fits! Here
it could not even be otherwise. What do the rules say about
it? Then the rules must be changed.

One should observe the curious structure of many themes,
even of shorter ones. The first theme of the Andante of the
Sixth Symphony, for example, is ten measures long. In constitution it is a period, which would normally be eight measures long. But in the fourth measure,

EXAMPLE 1

[21]

where the caesura would come in a period, the note G♭, which
can be a dotted quarter-note, as in Example 2,

EXAMPLE 2

is extended to three quarters; this shifts the eighth-note figure
|c| into the fifth measure. Thus the antecedent of the period
becomes four-and-a-half measures long. In a symmetrical
period the consequent is equally long; this would produce
nine measures in all. The consequent begins in the fifth
measure, and if a new extension, corresponding to the previous one, did not take place in the seventh measure, the
period would end, as in Example 3, in the ninth measure.

EXAMPLE 3

[22]

EXAMPLE 4

But it is not absolutely necessary for this melody to become ten measures long. Example 3 shows that in spite of the extension in the seventh measure an ending on the first beat of the ninth measure is possible. This indicates that in measures 8 and 9 there follows a further artificial extension, although cadential contraction already set in here.

It is amazing how these deviations from the conventional balance each other, even postulate each other. This demonstrates a highly developed feeling for form, such as one finds only in great masterpieces. This is not the *tour de force* of a "technician"—a master would not bring it off, if he made up his mind to it in advance. These are inspirations which escape the control of consciousness, inspirations which come only to the genius, who receives them unconsciously and formulates solutions without noticing that a problem has confronted him.

A well-known writer on music called Mahler's symphonies "gigantic symphonic potpourris." The term "potpourris" naturally applies to the banality of invention and not to the form, for "gigantically conceived" is supposed to apply to the form. Now, in the first place, there are also potpourris of classical music, from operas of Mozart, Wagner, etc. I do not know whether such a thing exists, but in any case it is easily conceivable that a potpourri could also consist of nothing but the most beautiful themes of Bach or Beethoven, without being anything but potpourri for all that. Therefore, the banality of the themes is not a significant feature of the potpourri. But in the second place, the characteristic of the potpourri is the unpretentiousness of the formal connectives. The individual sections are simply juxtaposed, without always being connected and without their relationships (which may also be entirely absent) being more than mere accidents in the form. But this is contradicted by the term "symphonic," which means the opposite. It means that the individual sections are organic components of a living being, born of a creative impulse and conceived as a whole. But this phrase, which really has no meaning in itself, which falls apart because it is thrice contradictory—this phrase became all the rage in Germany. In Vienna, where the worst evils are always possible in the press, someone even found it necessary to cite it in Mahler's obituary.

I find that quite fair. For the great artist must somehow be punished in his lifetime for the honor which he will enjoy later.

And the esteemed music critic must somehow be compensated in his lifetime for the contempt with which later times will treat him.

The only thing which everyone admitted to be valid in Mahler was his orchestration. That sounds suspicious, and one might almost believe that this praise, because it is so unanimous, is just as unfair as the abovementioned unanimities. And, in fact, Mahler never altered anything in the form of his compositions, but he was always changing the instrumentation. He seems to have felt that this was imperfect. It is certainly not, it is certainly of the highest perfection, and only the anxiety of the man who, as a conductor, had to strive for a clarity which he, as a composer, certainly did not find so necessary—since music assures the divine prerogative of anonymity of feelings, of obscurity for the uninitiated—only this anxiety drove him ever to seek, as a substitute for the perfect, the more perfect. But that does not exist. In any case, it is indicative that he was rather mistrustful of this universal praise. And it is a wonderful characteristic of great men that they view praise as fitting to them, but endure it even less patiently than they endure blame. But there is something more. I am firmly convinced that if one asks those

GUSTAV MAHLER

who praise Mahler's orchestration just what they mean,
they will name something that he would have disliked. There
is even proof of this; nearly everyone who orchestrates today
orchestrates well—if you read the critics. And there is certainly a difference between this good orchestration and
Mahler's thinking for orchestra!

What first strikes one about Mahler's instrumentation is
the almost unexampled objectivity with which he writes down
only what is absolutely necessary. His sound never comes from
ornamental additions, from accessories that are related not at
all or only distantly to the important material, and that are
put down only as decorations. But where it soughs, it is the
theme which soughs; the themes have such a form and so
many notes that it immediately becomes clear that the sough-
ing is not the *aim* of this passage, but its *form* and its *content*. Where it grunts and groans, the themes and harmonies
grunt and groan; but where it crashes, gigantic structures
clash against one another; the architecture crumbles; the
architectonic relationships of tension and pressure are in re-
volt. But among the most beautiful sounds are the delicate,
fragrant ones. Here, too, he brings unheard-of novelty, as,
for example, in the middle movements of the Seventh Symphony, with their sonorities of guitar, harp, and solo instruments. This guitar in the Seventh is not introduced for a
single effect, but the whole movement is based on this sonority. It belongs to it from the very beginning, it is a
living organ of the composition: not the heart, but perhaps
the eyes, whose glance is so characteristic of its aspect. This
instance is very close—in a more modern way, naturally—
to the method of the classical composers, who built whole
movements or pieces on the sonority of a specific instrumental group.

Probably we shall soon find out in detail that (and how)
Mahler, in such ways, is much closer to classical music than
he appears to be. Today it is not always easy to recognize
this, and naturally it is not always true. On the contrary,

up to a certain degree he must depart from it, because he progresses beyond it. But he goes beyond it not so much in forms, proportions, and extent, which are only the outer consequences of the inner happenings, as in content. This does not mean that the content is greater, more significant or more earth-shaking than in the works of other great masters, for there is only one content, which all great men wish to express: the longing of mankind for its future form, for an immortal soul, for dissolution into the universe—the longing of this soul for its God. This alone, though reached by many different roads and detours and expressed by many different means, is the content of the works of the great; and with all their strength, with all their will they yearn for it so long and desire it so intensely until it is accomplished. And this longing is transmitted with its full intensity from the predecessor to the successor, and the successor continues not only the content but also the intensity, adding proportionally to his heritage. This heritage carries responsibility, but it is imposed only upon one who can assume this responsibility.

It seems to me almost petty that I should speak of the conductor Mahler in the same breath as the composer. Not only was he always appreciated as a conductor even by the most stupid opponents, but one might also consider that the purely reproductive activity would be of merely secondary importance in comparison with the creative activity. But there are two reasons which induce me to take up this discussion. In the first place, nothing about a great man is secondary. Actually, every one of his acts is somehow productive. In this sense, I should even have liked to observe how Mahler knotted his tie, and should have found that more interesting and instructive than learning how one of our musical bigwigs composes on a "sacred subject." But, in the second place, it seems to me as if even this activity has not yet been completely comprehended in its most important aspect. Certainly, many have extolled his demonic personality, his unheard-of sense of style, the precision of his performances as well as their tonal beauty and clarity. But, for example, among other things I heard one of his "colleagues" say that there is no special trick to bringing off good performances when one has so many rehearsals. Certainly there is no trick to it, for the oftener one plays a thing through, the better it goes, and even the poorest conductors profit from this. But there is a trick to feeling the need for a tenth rehearsal during the ninth rehearsal because one still hears many things that can become better, *because one still knows something to say in the tenth rehearsal.* This is exactly the difference: a poor conductor often does not know what to do after the third rehearsal, he has nothing more to say, he is more easily satisfied, because he does not have the capacity for further discrimination, and because nothing in him imposes higher requirements. And this is the cause: the productive man conceives within himself a complete image of what he wishes to reproduce; the performance, like everything else that he brings forth, must not be less perfect than the image. Such re-creation is only slightly different from creation; virtually, only the approach is different. Only when one has clarified this point to oneself does one comprehend how much is meant by the modest words with which Mahler himself characterized his highest aim as a conductor: "I consider it my greatest service that I force the musicians to play exactly what is in the notes." That sounds almost too simple, too slight, to us; and in fact it is so, for we might ascribe the effects which we knew to far more profound causes. But if one imagines how precise must be the image engendered by the notes in one who is creative, and what sensitivity is necessary in order to distinguish whether the reality and the image correspond to one another; if one thinks of what is necessary in order to express these fine distinctions so understandably that the performing musician, while merely playing the right notes, now suddenly participates in the spirit of the music as well—then one understands that with these modest words everything has been said.

This modesty was so characteristic of Mahler. Never a movement which was not exactly consistent with its cause! It was just as large as it had to be; it was executed with temperament, with life, energetically, powerfully, for temperament is the executive of conviction, and it will never be inactive. But there were no outbreaks without cause—none of that false temperament which today brings such great success to those who imitate Mahler's earlier manner of conducting. When he conducted thus, turning with violent movements to individual instrumental groups, really acting out for them the power and force which they were to express, he had arrived at the boundary of manly maturity which still permits that sort of thing. When he had crossed the boundary, the change set in, and he conducted the orchestra with unexampled composure. All exertion took place in the rehearsals, the violent gestures disappeared, ever greater clarity of the power of verbal expression replaced them. Here a young man had passed into maturity, and did not strive to retain the gestures of youth, because he never deceived, but always did what was fitting to his situation. But he would never have conducted quietly while he was young; the rubato corresponded to his youth, the steadiness to his maturity. And let it be said to those younger conductors who today imitate Mahlerian composure that this is not in his spirit. His was a different concept. To emulate him means always to be as one's own feelings dictate. The other thing is mere aping. For him there were no other rules than these, and no models for him to imitate. One has to live up to one's models. But that takes courage. This Mahler possessed in the highest degree. Nothing could keep him from taking the utmost risks for what he deemed to be necessary. This was shown by his direction of the Vienna Opera, and by the enemies whom he won for himself because of it. He unified all the worst people in Vienna; the most unreliable ones were tied down, became fighters against him for a dead certainty. But he also had the courage to endure, to be patient. He was innocently involved in an affair, in spite of which he took the assaults of the press without batting an eyelash, because in order to answer them he would have had to sacrifice a younger friend, and he did not want to do that. Smiling, he took the whole thing as a matter of course, and never breathed a word of it later.

In Vienna, as director of the Imperial Opera, he did not serve as a musician alone. He not only demanded from musicians and singers an approach to perfection and selfless devotion to the will of the masterworks, but he was also their interpreter in the explanation of the poetic content. How deeply his thinking penetrated into the intent of the masters may be illustrated by the following example.

In a conversation about Wagner's poems I observed that I was unable to decipher the deeper meaning of the text of *Lohengrin*. The mere tale, with its romantic wonders, curses, bewitchments, magic potions, and metamorphoses, did not seem to correspond to deeper human feelings. In spite of the great impression made by the summons to patriotism and by the consecration of the Grail, it was hard to blame Elsa for wanting to know Lohengrin's origin, even if Ortrud had not aroused her suspicion.

"It is the difference between man and woman," explained Mahler. "Elsa is the skeptical woman. She is incapable of having the same degree of confidence in the man that he showed when he fought for her, believing in her without questioning her guilt or innocence. The capacity for trust is masculine, suspicion is feminine." Certainly, suspicion originates in the fear of the one who needs protection, while trust results from the sense of power of her protector, the protector of Brabant. This interpretation reveals the deeply human background of the rather theatrical "Nie sollst du mich befragen."

Mahler, a man racked with passion, who had gone through

all the storms of life, who had been hounded by friends, who had himself exalted and overthrown gods, at the climax of his life possessed that composure, that moderation, that perspective, which he obtained by purification of the mind from dross. This enabled him always to see the most profound aspect of the works of the great; upon this was based an unswerving respect, which we younger men were on the way to losing.

Mahler was no friend of program music. Though he—an autocrat—did not like to discuss such things, he did not like it any better when people, flattering, would say what they assumed he would like. A younger conductor had to experience this when, in addition, he made one more mistake in attacking Wagner. "The words of Wagner that you quote are entirely clear to me," he wrote; "that our music reflects the purely human (and everything that goes with it, including the intellectual) in one way or another cannot be denied. As in all art, it is a matter of appropriate means of expression! But what one puts into music is always the *whole*, feeling, thinking, breathing, suffering man." Against this, he continued, there need be no objection if a musician expresses himself therein—but not a poet, a philosopher, a painter!

Such wisdom protected him from exaggeration. Apostles are often more papistical than the Pope, because they lack the proper moderation. He knew that one thing is not absolutely false in itself any more than its opposite is absolutely true in itself. Therefore, his deeply rooted cognition of real values would not permit fitting respect to be denied to one of the truly great. Perhaps this reaction originated in his code of honor, just as every officer will immediately, under all circumstances, revenge an insult to another officer.

This happened to me. In my development there was a phase during which I took a negative, even an inimical stand against Wagner, whom I had previously honored with the highest. It seems that I expressed myself about it to Mahler with violent and arrogant words. Although visibly shocked, he replied with impressive calm that he knew such states of mind, he too had passed through such stages of development. This would be nothing lasting; for one always comes back again and again to the truly great ones. They stand unshakably in their places and it is commendable never to lose our respect for them.

This reprimand was of great consequence to me ever afterwards, for it became clear to me that only he is capable of respect who deserves respect himself, and that this sentence could even be inverted: he who cannot respect another is himself unworthy of respect. And this realization is especially important today, when social climbers belittle a great man in order to seem greater themselves.

I have tried to define the difference between genius and talent as follows:

Talent is the capacity to learn, genius the capacity to develop oneself. Talent grows by acquiring capacities which already existed outside of itself; it assimilates these, and finally even possesses them. Genius already possesses all its future faculties from the very beginning. It only develops them; it merely unwinds, unrolls, unfolds them. While talent, which has to master a limited material (namely, what is already given) very soon reaches its apex and then usually subsides, the development of the genius, which seeks new pathways into the boundless, extends throughout a lifetime. And therefore it comes about that no one single moment in this development is like another. Each stage is simultaneously a preparation for the next stage. It is an eternal metamorphosis, an uninterrupted growth of new shoots from a single kernel. It is then clear why two widely separated points in this development are so strangely different from each other that at first one does not recognize how much they belong together. Only on closer study does one perceive in the potentialities of the earlier period the certainties of the later one.

The pictures of Mahler furnish me with remarkable proof of this statement.

Here is one which shows him at the age of about eighteen. Everything is still unrevealed. This is a youth who still does not foresee what will take place within him. He does not look like those young artists to whom it is more important to look great than to be great. He looks like one who is waiting for something which is about to happen, but which he does not yet know about. A second picture shows him about twenty-five years old. Here something has already taken place. Curiously, the forehead has become higher; the brain obviously takes up more room. And the features! Formerly, in spite of all their striking seriousness, they were almost those of one who wants to gather a little more strength before he sets to work; now they are tense. They betray that he already knows the good and evil of the world, but they are almost arrogant; he will soon make all of them look small. But now we skip to the head of the fifty-year-old man. This development seems miraculous. It shows almost no resemblance to the youthful pictures. The development from within has given it a form which, I might say, has swallowed up all the previous phases. Certainly they too are contained in the final form. Certainly anyone who can see has already detected the whole man in the youthful pictures. But, when one looks backwards at the earlier stages— though they themselves are certainly expressive, it is as difficult to discover the expression of the mature man in them as it is to see the beams of a lesser light next to a very bright one. One must avert one's eyes from the certainties of the older face for a long time before one can again see the potentialities in the younger one. Here the thoughts and feelings that moved this man have created a form. This is not what happens to the young geniuses who look their best when they are young, and who turn into Philistines, even outwardly and visibly, when they grow older. One cannot learn one's appearance. And what one has learned does not remain, but goes away. But what is inborn goes from one climax to the next, develops itself to ever higher forms of expression. It makes leaps which become more enigmatic to the observer the more urgently he desires to understand them. Mahler's development is one of the most overwhelming ones. Actually, everything which will characterize him is already present in the First Symphony; here already his life-melody begins, and he merely develops it, unfolds it to the utmost extent. Here are his devotion to nature and his thoughts of death. He is still struggling with fate here, but in the Sixth he acknowledges it, and this acknowledgment is resignation. But even resignation becomes productive, and rises, in the Eighth, to the glorification of the highest joys, to a glorification only possible to one who already knows that these joys are no longer for him; who has already resigned himself; who already feels that they are merely an allegory for ever higher joys, a glorification of the most supreme bliss, as he also expresses it verbally in the letter to his wife where he explains the final scenes of *Faust*:

"*All that is passing* (what I performed for you on those two evenings) is but a *likeness;* naturally, inadequate in its earthly appearance—*but there,* freed from the corporeality of earthly insufficiency, it will become *real,* and then we need no more paraphrases, no more comparisons—likenesses— *there has already been done* what I tried to describe here, which is *simply indescribable.* And what is it? Again, I can tell you only through a comparison:

The Eternal Feminine has drawn us upward—we are there —we are at rest—we possess what we on earth could only long for, strive for....."

That is one way to reach the goal! Not just with the understanding, but with the feeling that one already lives there *oneself.* He who looks on the earth thus no longer lives upon it. He has already been drawn upwards.

In musical matters, Mahler's development exhibits an uninterrupted ascent. Certainly, the first symphonies already display great formal perfection. But when one thinks of the tautness and compactness of the form of the Sixth, where there is no superfluous note, where even the most far-reaching extension is an essential part of the whole and is fitted in organically; when one tries to comprehend that the two movements of the Eighth are nothing else than a single idea of unheard-of length and breadth, a single idea conceived, surveyed and mastered in the same moment—then one wonders at the power of a mind which could already trust itself for unbelievable feats in its young years but which has made real the most improbable.

And then in *Das Lied von der Erde* he is suddenly capable of producing the briefest and most delicate forms. This is most extraordinary, but understandable: infinity in the Eighth, the finite nature of earthly things in this work.

His Ninth is most strange. In it, the author hardly speaks as an individual any longer. It almost seems as though this work must have a concealed author who used Mahler merely as his spokesman, as his mouthpiece. This symphony is no longer couched in the personal tone. It consists, so to speak, of objective, almost passionless statements of a beauty which becomes perceptible only to one who can dispense with animal warmth and feels at home in spiritual coolness. We shall know as little about what his Tenth (for which, as also in the case of Beethoven, sketches exist) would have said as we know about Beethoven's or Bruckner's. It seems that the Ninth is a limit. He who wants to go beyond it must pass away. It seems as if something might be imparted to us in the Tenth which we ought not yet to know, for which we are not yet ready. Those who have written a Ninth stood too near to the hereafter. Perhaps the riddles of this world would be solved, if one of those who knew them were to write a Tenth. And that probably is not to take place.

We are still to remain in a darkness which will be illuminated only fitfully by the light of genius. We are to continue to battle and struggle, to yearn and desire. And it is to be denied us to see this light as long as it remains with us. We are to remain blind until we have acquired eyes. Eyes that see the future. Eyes that penetrate more than the sensual, which is only a likeness; that penetrate the supersensual. Our soul shall be the eye. We have a duty: to win for ourselves an immortal soul. It is promised to us. We already possess it in the future; we must bring it about that this future becomes our present. That we live in this future alone, and not in a present which is only a likeness, and which, as every likeness, is inadequate.

And this is the essence of genius—that it is the future. This is why the genius is nothing to the present. Because present and genius have nothing to do with one another. The genius is our future. So shall we too be one day, when we have fought our way through. The genius lights the way, and we strive to follow. Where he is, the light is already bright; but we cannot endure this brightness. We are blinded, and see only a reality which is as yet no reality, which is only the present. But a higher reality is lasting, and the present passes away. The future is eternal, and therefore the higher reality, the reality of our immortal soul, exists only in the future.

The genius lights the way, and we strive to follow. Do we really strive enough? Are we not bound too much to the present?

We shall follow, for we must. Whether we want to or not. It draws us upward.

We must follow.

This, it seems to me, is what Gustav Mahler's work, like the work of every great man, was allowed to tell us. It has been told us often, and will have to be told us much oftener still before we grasp it completely. It always becomes very quiet after one of these great men has spoken. We listen. But soon life overwhelms us again with its noise.

Mahler was allowed to reveal just so much of this future; when he wanted to say more, he was called away. For it is not to become entirely quiet yet; there is to be still more battle and noise.

And we are still to glow with the reflection of a light which would blind us if we saw it.

I have fought here for Mahler and his work. But I have indulged in polemics, I have spoken hard and sharp words against his opponents. I know that if he were listening he would smile and wave it away. For he is where retaliation is no longer practised.

But we must fight on, since the Tenth has not yet been revealed to us.

New Music, Outmoded Music, Style and Idea

THE FIRST three of these four concepts have been widely used in the last twenty-five years, while not so much ado has been made about the fourth, *idea*.

Unfortunately, methods in music teaching, instead of making students thoroughly acquainted with the music itself, furnish a conglomerate of more or less true historical facts, sugarcoated with a great number of more or less false anecdotes about the composer, his performers, his audiences, and his critics, plus a strong dose of popularized esthetics. Thus I once read in an examination paper of a sophomore, who had studied only a little harmony and much music appreciation, but who had certainly not heard much "live" music, that "Schumann's orchestration is gloomy and unclear." This wisdom was derived directly and verbally from the textbook used in class. Some experts on orchestration might agree upon the condemnation of Schumann as an orchestrator, perhaps even without an argument. However, there might be other experts who would agree that not all of Schumann's orchestration is poor—that there are gloomy spots as well as brilliant or at least good ones; they would also know that this accusation stems from the fight between the Wagnerian "New-German" School and the Schumann-Brahmsian-Academic-Classicist School, and that the critics had in mind such brilliant parts of Wagner's music as the "Magic Fire," the *Meistersinger* Overture, the *Venusberg* music and others. Such brilliancy can but seldom be found in Schumann's music. But some experts also know that there are very few compositions whose orchestration is perfectly flawless. More than two decades after Wagner's death, for instance, his orchestral accompaniment covered the singers' voices so as to make them inaudible. I know that Gustav Mahler had to change his orchestration very much for the sake of transparency. And Strauss himself showed me several cases where he had to make adjustment.

Thus, there is not the same degree of unanimity among experts of orchestration as there is between the sophomore girl and her textbook. But irreparable damage has been done; this girl, and probably all her classmates, will never listen to the orchestra of Schumann naively, sensitively, and open-mindedly. At the end of the term she will have acquired a knowledge of music history, esthetics, and criticism, plus a number of amusing anecdotes; but unfortunately she may not remember even one of those gloomily orchestrated Schumann themes. In a few years she will take her master's degree in music, or will have become a teacher, or both, and will disseminate what she has been taught: ready-made judgments, wrong and superficial ideas about music, musicians, and esthetics.

In this manner there are educated a great number of pseudo-historians who believe themselves to be experts and, as such, entitled not only to criticize music and musicians, but even to usurp the role of leaders, to gain influence in the development of the art of music and to organize it in advance.

A few years after the first World War, such pseudo-historians acquired a dominant voice, throughout Western Europe, in predicting the future of music. In all music-producing countries, in France, Italy, Germany, Austria, Hungary, Czechoslovakia and Poland, there suddenly arose the slogan:

"NEW MUSIC"

This battle-cry had evidently been created because one of these pseudo-historians had remembered that several times in the past the same battle-cry, or others like it, had furthered a new direction in the arts. A battle-cry must, perhaps, be superficial and at least partially wrong if it is to gain popularity. Thus we may understand Schopenhauer's story of the surprise of one ancient Greek orator who, when he was suddenly interrupted by applause and cheers, cried out: "Have I said some nonsense?" The popularity acquired by this slogan, "New Music," immediately arouses suspicion and forces one to question its meaning.

What is New Music?

Evidently it must be music which, though it is still music, differs in all essentials from previously composed music. Evidently it must express something which has not yet been expressed in music. Evidently, in higher art, only that is worth being presented which has never before been presented. There is no great work of art which does not convey a new message to humanity; there is no great artist who fails in this respect. This is the code of honor of all the great in art, and consequently in all great works of the great we will find that newness which never perishes, whether it be of Josquin des Prés, of Bach or Haydn, or of any other great master.

Because: *Art means New Art.*

The idea that this slogan "New Music" might change the course of musical production was probably based on the belief that "history repeats itself." As everybody knows, while Bach still was living a new musical style came into being out of which there later grew the style of the Viennese Classicists, the style of homophonic-melodic composition, or, as I call it, the style of Developing Variation. If, then, history really repeated itself, the assumption that one need only demand the creation of new music would also suffice in our time, and at once the ready-made product would be served.

This is mistaking symptoms for causes. The real causes of changes in the style of musical composition are others. If in a period of homophonic composition musicians had acquired great skill in creating melodies—that is, main voices which reduced accompanying voices to almost meaningless inferiority in order to concentrate all possible contents in themselves—other composers may well have been annoyed by such a skill, which seemed already to degenerate into a schematic mechanism. They may then have been even more annoyed by the inferiority of the accompaniment than by what seemed to them the sweetness of the melody. While in this period only one direction of the musical space, the horizontal line, had been developed, the composers of the next period might have responded to a tendency that demanded the vitalizing of the accompanying voices also—that is, following the vertical direction of the musical space. Such tendencies might have provoked that richer elaboration of the accompaniment seen, for instance, in Beethoven as compared with Haydn, Brahms as compared with Mozart, or Wagner as compared with Schumann. Though in all these cases the richness of the melody has not suffered in the least, the role of the accompaniment has been intensified, enhancing its contribution to the common effect. No historian need tell a Beethoven, a Brahms, a Wagner to enrich his accompaniment with vitamins. At least these three men, stubborn as they were, would have shown him the door!

And vice-versa:

If, in a given period, each participating voice had been elaborated, with respect to its content, its formal balance and its relation to other voices, as part of a contrapuntal combination, its share of melodic eloquence would be less than if it were the main voice. Again, there might then arise in younger composers a longing to get rid of all these complexities. They then might refuse to deal with combinations and elaborations of subordinate voices. Thus the desire to elaborate only one voice and reduce the accompaniment to that minimum required by comprehensibility would again be the ruling fashion.

Such are the causes which produce changes in methods of composition. In a manifold sense, music uses time. It uses my time, it uses your time, it uses its own time. It would be most annoying if it did not aim to say the most important things in the most concentrated manner in every fraction of this time. This is why, when composers have acquired the technique of filling one direction with content to the utmost capacity, they must do the same in the next direction, and finally in all the directions in which music expands. Such progress can occur only step-wise. The necessity of compromising with comprehensibility forbids jumping into a style which is overcrowded with content, a style in which facts are too often juxtaposed without connectives, and which leaps to conclusions before proper maturation.

If music abandoned its former direction and turned towards new goals in this manner, I doubt that the men who produced this change needed the exhortation of pseudo-historians. We know that they—the Telemanns, the Couperins, the Rameaus, the Keysers, the Ph. E. Bachs and others—created something new which led only later to the period of the Viennese Classicists. Yes, a new style in music was created, but did this have the consequence of making the music of the preceding period outmoded?

Curiously, it happened at the beginning of this period that J. S. Bach's music was called outmoded. And, most curiously, one of those who said this was J. S. Bach's own son, Ph. Emanuel Bach, whose greatness one might question if one did not know that Mozart and Beethoven viewed him with great admiration. To them, he still seemed a leader, even after they themselves had added to the first rather negative principles of the New Music such positive principles as that of developing variation, in addition to many hitherto unknown structural devices such as those of transition, liquidation, dramatic recapitulation, manifold elaboration, derivation of subordinate themes, highly differentiated dynamics—*crescendo, decrescendo, sforzato, piano subito, marcato,* etc.— and particularly the new technique of *legato* and *staccato* passages, *accelerando* and *ritardando,* and the establishment of tempo and character by specific bywords.

Beethoven's words: "Das ist nicht ein Bach, das ist ein Meer" (This is not a brook, this is an ocean) constitute the correct order. He did not say this about Philipp Emanuel but about Johann Sebastian. Should he not have added: Who is the brook?

In any case:

While until 1750 J. S. Bach was writing countless works whose originality seems the more astonishing to us the more we study his music; while he not only developed but really created a new style of music which was without precedent; while the very nature of this newness still escapes the observation of the experts—

No, excuse me: I feel obliged to prove what I say, and hate to say it as lightly and superficially as if I were to say: New Music!

The newness of Bach's art can only be understood by comparing it with the style of the Netherlands School on the one hand and with Handel's art on the other.

The secrets of the Netherlanders, strictly denied to the uninitiated, were based on a complete recognition of the possible contrapuntal relations between the seven tones of the diatonic scale. This enabled the initiated to produce combinations which admitted many types of vertical and horizontal shifts, and other similar changes. But the remaining five tones were not included in these rules, and, if they appeared at all, did so apart from the contrapuntal combination and as occasional substitutes.

In contrast, Bach, who knew more secrets than the Netherlanders ever possessed, enlarged these rules to such an extent that they comprised all the twelve tones of the chromatic scale. Bach sometimes operated with the twelve tones in such a manner that one would be inclined to call him the first twelve-tone composer.

If, after observing that the contrapuntal flexibility of Bach's themes is based in all probability on his instinctive thinking in terms of multiple counterpoint which gives scope to additional voices, one compares his counterpoint with Handel's, the latter's seems bare and simple, and his subordinate voices are really inferior.

Also in other respects Bach's art is higher than Handel's. As a composer for the theatre Handel always had the power of beginning with a characteristic and often excellent theme. But, thereafter, with the exception of the repetitions of the theme, there follows a decline, bringing only what the editor of *Grove's Dictionary* would call "trash"—empty, meaningless, etude-like broken chord figures. In contrast, even Bach's transitional and subordinate sections are always full of character, inventiveness, imagination and expression. Though his subordinate voices never degenerate into inferiority, he is able to write fluent and well balanced melodies of more beauty, richness and expressiveness than can be found in the music of all those Keysers, Telemanns, and Philipp Emanuel Bachs who called him outmoded. They, of course, were not capable of seeing that he was also the first to introduce just that technique so necessary for the progress of their New Music: the technique of "developing variation," which made possible the style of the great Viennese Classicists.

While Bach thus—as beforementioned—produced work after work in a new style, his contemporaries knew no better than to ignore him. It can be said that not much of their New Music remained alive, though one must not deny that it was the beginning of a new art. But there are two points in which they were wrong. First, it was not musical *ideas* which their New Music wanted to establish, but only a new style for the presentation of musical ideas, whether old or new; it was a new wave in the progress of music, one which, as described before, tried to develop the other direction of musical space, the horizontal line. Second, they were wrong when they called Bach's music outmoded. At least it was not outmoded forever, as history shows; today their New Music is outmoded while Bach's has become eternal.

But now one should also examine the concept "outmoded."

One can find illustrations of this concept in our daily life rather than in the intellectual sphere. Long hair, for instance, was considered an important contribution to a woman's beauty thirty years ago. Who knows how soon the fashion of short hair will be outmoded? Pathos was one of the most admired merits of poetry about a hundred years ago; today it seems ridiculous, and it is used only for satirical purposes. Electric light has outmoded candle-light; but snobs still use the latter because they saw it in the castles of the aristocracy where artistically decorated walls would have been damaged by electric wiring.

Does this indicate why things become outmoded?

Long hair became outmoded because working women considered it a handicap. Pathos became outmoded when naturalism portrayed real life and the way in which people talked when they wanted to finish business. Candle-light became outmoded when people realized how senseless it is to make unnecessary work for one's servants—if one can get them at all.

The common factor in all these examples was a change in the forms of our life.

Can one contend the same about music?

Which form of life makes Romantic music inadequate? Is there no more romanticism in our time? Are we not more enthusiastic about being killed by our automobiles than the ancient Romans were about being killed by their chariots? Are there not still to be found young people who engage in adventure for which they may have to pay with their lives, though the glory they earn will pale with the next day's front page? Would it not be easy to find numerous youths to fly to the moon in a rocket plane if the opportunity were offered? Is not the admiration of people of all ages for our Tarzans, Supermen, Lone Rangers and indestructible detectives the result of a love for romanticism? The Indian stories of our youth were no more romantic; only the names of the subjects have been changed.

One reproach against romanticism concerns its complications. True, if one were to look at scores of Strauss, Debussy, Mahler, Ravel, Reger, or my own, it might be difficult to decide whether all this complication is necessary. But the decision of one successful young composer: "Today's younger generation does not like music which they do not understand," does not conform to the feelings of the heroes who engage in adventures. One might expect that this kind of youth, attracted by the difficult, the dangerous, the mysterious, would rather say: "Am I an idiot that one dares offer me poor trash which I understand before I am half-way through?" Or even: "This music is complicated, but I will not give up until I understand it." Of course this kind of man will be enthused rather by profundity, profuseness of ideas, difficult problems. Intelligent people have always been offended if one bothered them with matters which any idiot could understand at once.

The reader has certainly become aware that it is not merely my intention to attack long deceased pseudo-historians and the composers who started the movement of New Music. Though I have used with pleasure the opportunity to write about some of the lesser known merits of Bach's art, and though I have enjoyed the opportunity to list some of the contributions of the Viennese Classicists to the development of compositorial technique, I do not hesitate to admit that the attack upon the propagandists of the New Music is aimed against similar movements in our own time. Except for one difference—that I am no Bach—there is a great similarity between the two epochs.

A superficial judgment might consider composition with twelve tones as an end to the period in which chromaticism evolved, and thus compare it to the climaxing end of the period of contrapuntal composition which Bach set by his unsurpassable mastery. That only lesser values could follow this climax is a kind of justification of his younger contemporaries' turn towards New Music.

But—also in this respect I am no Bach—I believe that composition with twelve tones and what many erroneously call "atonal music" is not the end of an old period, but the beginning of a new one. Again, as two centuries ago, something is called outmoded; and again it is not one particular work, or several works of one composer; again it is not the greater or lesser ability of one composer in particular; but again it is a style which has become ostracized. Again it calls itself New Music, and this time even more nations participate in the struggle. Aside from nationalistic aims for an exportable music with which even smaller nations hope to conquer the market, there is one common trait observable in all these movements; none of them are occupied with presenting new ideas, but only with presenting a new style. And, again, the principles on which this New Music is to be based present themselves even more negatively than the strictest rules of the strictest old counterpoint. There should be avoided: chromaticism, expressive melodies, Wagnerian harmonies, romanticism, private biographical hints, subjectivity, functional harmonic progressions, illustrations, leitmotivs, concurrence with the mood or action of the scene and characteristic declamation of the text in opera, songs and choruses. In other words, all that was good in the preceding period should not occur now.

Besides these officially authorized "Verbote," I have observed numerous negative merits, such as: pedal points (instead of elaborate bass voices and moving harmony), ostinatos, sequences (instead of developing variation), fugatos (for similar purposes), dissonances (disguising the vulgarity of the thematic material), objectivity (*Neue Sachlichkeit*), and a kind of polyphony, substituting for counterpoint, which, because of its inexact imitations, in former times would have been held in contempt as "Kapellmeistermusik," or what I called "Rhabarber counterpoint." The word "Rhabarber," spoken behind the scenes by only five or six people, sounded to the audience in a theatre like a rioting mob. Thus the counterpoint, thematically meaningless, like the word "rhubarb," sounded as if it had a real meaning.

In my youth, living in the proximity of Brahms, it was

customary that a musician, when he heard a composition the first time, observed its construction, was able to follow the elaboration and derivation of its themes and its modulations, and could recognize the number of voices in canons and the presence of the theme in a variation; and there were even laymen who after one hearing could take a melody home in their memory. But I am sure there was not much talk about style. And if a music historian had ventured to participate in an argument, it could only have been one who was able to observe similar qualities by ear alone. That is what music critics like Hanslick, Kalbeck, Heuberger and Speidel and amateurs like the renowned physician Billroth were able to do.

The positive and negative rules may be deduced from a finished work as constituents of its style. Every man has finger-prints of his own, and every craftsman's hand has its person-ality; out of such subjectivity grow the traits which comprise the style of the finished product. Every craftsman is limited by the shortcomings of his hands but is furthered by their particular abilities. On his natural conditions depends the style of everything he does, and so it would be wrong to expect a plum tree to bear plums of glass or pears or felt hats. Among all trees it is only the Christmas tree which bears fruits not natural to it, and among animals it is only the Easter rabbit which lays eggs, and even colored ones at that.

Style is the quality of a work and is based on natural conditions, expressing him who produced it. In fact, one who knows his capacities may be able to tell in advance exactly how the finished work will look which he still sees only in his imagination. But he will never start from a preconceived image of a style; he will be ceaselessly occupied with doing justice to the idea. He is sure that, everything done which the idea demands, the external appearance will be adequate.

If I have been fortunate enough to show some views different from those of my adversaries about New Music, Outmoded Music, and Style, I would like to proceed now to my self-appointed task of discussing what seems to me most important in a work of art—the Idea.

I am conscious that entering into this sphere involves some danger. Adversaries have called me a constructor, an engineer, an architect, even a mathematician—not to flatter me—because of my method of composing with twelve tones. In spite of knowing my *Verklärte Nacht* and *Gurre-Lieder,* though some people liked these works because of their emotionality, they called my music dry and denied me spontaneity. They pretended that I offered the products of a brain, not of a heart.

I have often wondered whether people who possess a brain would prefer to hide this fact. I have been supported in my own attitude by the example of Beethoven who, having received a letter from his brother Johann signed "land owner," signed his reply "brain owner." One might question why Beethoven just stressed the point of owning a brain. He had so many other merits to be proud of, for instance, being able to compose music which some people considered outstanding, being an accomplished pianist—and, as such, even recognized by the nobility—and being able to satisfy his publishers by giving them something of value for their money. Why did he call himself just "brain owner," when the possession of a brain is considered a danger to the naiveté of an artist by many pseudo-historians?

An experience of mine might illustrate the way in which people think a brain might be dangerous. I have never found it necessary to hide that I am able to think logically, that I distinguish sharply between right and wrong terms, and that I have very exact ideas about what art should be. Thus, in a number of discussions, I may have shown a little too much brain to one of my tennis partners, a writer of lyric poetry. He did not reciprocate in kind, but maliciously told me the story about the toad who asked the centipede whether he was always conscious which of his hundred feet was just about to move, whereupon the centipede, in becoming conscious of the necessary decision, lost his instinctive ability to walk at all.

Indeed, a great danger to a composer! And even hiding his brain might not help; only having none would suffice. But I think this need not discourage anyone who has a brain; because I have observed that if one has not worked hard enough and has not done one's best, the Lord will refuse to add His blessing. He has given us a brain in order to use it. Of course an idea is not always the product of brain-work. Ideas may invade the mind as unprovoked and perhaps even as undesired as a musical sound reaches the ear or an odor the nose.

Ideas can only be honored by one who has some of his own; but only he can do honor who deserves honor himself.

The difference between style and idea in music has perhaps been clarified by the preceding discussion. This may not be the place to discuss in detail what idea in itself means in music, because almost all musical terminology is vague and most of its terms are used in various meanings. In its most common meaning, the term idea is used as a synonym for theme, melody, phrase or motive. I myself consider the totality of a piece as the *idea*: the idea which its creator wanted to present. But because of the lack of better terms I am forced to define the term idea in the following manner:

Every tone which is added to a beginning tone makes the meaning of that tone doubtful. If, for instance, G follows after C, the ear may not be sure whether this expresses C major or G major, or even F major or E minor; and the addition of other tones may or may not clarify this problem. In this manner there is produced a state of unrest, of imbalance which grows throughout most of the piece, and is enforced further by similar functions of the rhythm. The method by which balance is restored seems to me the real *idea* of the composition. Perhaps the frequent repetitions of themes, groups, and even larger sections might be considered as attempts towards an early balance of the inherent tension.

In comparison with all our developments in mechanics, a tool like a pair of pliers might seem simple. I always admired the mind which invented it. In order to understand the problem which this inventor had to overcome one must imagine the state of mechanics before its invention. The idea of fixing the crosspoint of the two crooked arms so that the two smaller segments in front would move in the opposite direction to the larger segments at the back, thus multiplying the power of the man who squeezed them to such an extent that he could cut wire—this idea can only have been conceived by a genius. Certainly more complicated and better tools exist today, and there may come a time when the use of the pliers and other similar tools may become superfluous. The tool itself may fall into disuse, but the idea behind it can never become obsolete. And therein lies the difference between a mere style and a real idea.

An idea can never perish.

It is very regrettable that so many contemporary composers care so much about style and so little about idea. From this came such notions as the attempt to compose in ancient styles, using their mannerisms, limiting oneself to the little that one can thus express and to the insignificance of the musical configurations which can be produced with such equipment.

No one should give in to limitations other than those which are due to the limits of his talent. No violinist would play, even occcasionally, with the wrong intonation to please lower musical tastes, no tight-rope walker would take steps in the wrong direction only for pleasure or for popular appeal, no chess master would make moves everyone could anticipate just to be agreeable (and thus allow his opponent to win), no mathematician would invent something new in mathematics just to flatter the masses who do not possess the specific mathematical way of thinking, and in the same manner, no artist, no poet, no philosopher and no musician whose thinking occurs in the highest sphere would degenerate into vulgarity in order to comply with a slogan such as "Art for All." Because if it is art, it is not for all, and if it is for all, it is not art.

Most deplorable is the acting of some artists who arrogantly wish to make believe that they descend from their heights in order to give some of their riches to the masses. This is hypocrisy. But there are a few composers, like Offenbach, Johann Strauss and Gershwin, whose feelings actually coincide with those of the "average man in the street." To them it is no masquerade to express popular feelings in popular terms. They are natural when they talk thus and about that.

He who really uses his brain for thinking can only be possessed of one desire: to resolve his task. He cannot let external conditions exert influence upon the results of his thinking. Two times two is four—whether one likes it or not.

One thinks only for the sake of one's idea.

And thus art can only be created for its own sake. An idea is born; it must be molded, formulated, developed, elaborated, carried through and pursued to its very end.

Because there is only "l'art pour l'art," art for the sake of art alone.

Brahms the Progressive [1]

I

IT HAS BEEN SAID that Brahms' social manners were often characterized by a certain dryness. This was not the "Unknown" Brahms.[2] Vienna knew his method of surrounding himself with a protective wall of stiffness as a defense against certain types of people, against the obtrusiveness of oily bombast, moist flattery, or honeyed impertinence. It is not unknown that those annoying bores, those sensationalists who were out for a good anecdote and those tactless intruders into private lives got little better than dryness. When the sluices of their eloquence were open and the flood threatened to engulf him, dryness was no protection. This is why he was often forced to resort to rudeness. Even so, his victims may have tacitly agreed to nickname what had befallen them "Brahmsian dryness"; and it may be assumed that each one rejoiced at the other's misfortune, but thought that he himself had been done wrong.

Dryness or rudeness, one thing is certain: Brahms did not want to express high esteem in this manner.

Contemporaries found various ways to annoy him. A musician or a music lover might intend to display his own great understanding, good judgment of music, and acquaintance with "some" of Brahms' music. Hence he dared say he had observed that Brahms' *First Piano Sonata* was very similar

---

[1] This essay was originally a lecture delivered in February, 1933, on the occasion of Brahms' 100th birthday. This year, 1933, was also the 50th anniversary of Wagner's death. This is a fully reformulated version of my original lecture. Many things and some of my opinions have changed during that time, and now 1947 is again an anniversary of Brahms; he died fifty years ago.

[2] As misrepresented by Robert Haven Schauffler in his book of the same name.

to Beethoven's *Hammerklavier* Sonata. No wonder that Brahms, in his straightforward manner, spoke out: "Das bemerkt ja schon jeder Esel." ("Every jackass notices that!")

A visitor meant to be complimentary when he said: "You are one of the greatest living composers." How Brahms hated this "one of." Who does not see that it means, "There are a few greater than you, and several of equivalent rank?"

But doubtless the most annoying were those visitors (like one composer from Berlin) who told him: "I am an admirer of Wagner, the progressive, the innovator, *and* of Brahms, the academician, the classicist." I do not remember what kind of dryness or rudeness he applied in this case, but I know there was a great story in Vienna about the manner in which Brahms presented his esteem for this flattery.

But, after all, it was the attitude of the time; those who disliked Wagner clung to Brahms, and vice versa. There were many who disliked both. They were, perhaps, the only non-partisans. Only a small number were able to disregard the polarity of these two contrasting figures while enjoying the beauties of both of them.

What in 1883 semed an impassable gulf was in 1897 no longer a problem. The greatest musicians of that time, Mahler, Strauss, Reger, and many others had grown up under the influence of both these masters. They all reflected the spiritual, emotional, stylistic and technical achievements of the preceding period. What then had been an object of dispute had been reduced into the difference between two personalities, between two styles of expression, not contradictory enough to prevent the inclusion of qualities of both in one work.

Form in Music serves to bring about comprehensibility through memorability. Evenness, regularity, symmetry, subdivision, repetition, unity, relationship in rhythm and harmony and even logic—none of these elements produces or even contributes to beauty. But all of them contribute to an organization which makes the presentation of the musical idea intelligible. The language in which musical ideas are ex-

[53]

pressed in tones parallels the language which expresses feelings or thoughts in words, in that its vocabulary must be proportionate to the intellect which it addresses, and in that the aforementioned elements of its organization function like the rhyme, the rhythm, the meter, and the subdivision into strophes, sentences, paragraphs, chapters, etc. in poetry or prose.

The more or less complete exploitation of the potency of these components determines the aesthetic value and the classification of the style in respect to its popularity or profundity. Science must explore and examine all facts; art is only concerned with the presentation of characteristic facts. Even Antony, when addressing the Roman people, realizes that he must repeat his ". . . and Brutus is an honorable man" over and over, if this contrast is to penetrate into the minds of simple citizens. Repetitions in Mother Goose songs are of course on a different level, and so is the organization of popular music. Here one finds numerous slightly varied repetitions, as in the otherwise very beautiful *Blue Danube Waltz*.

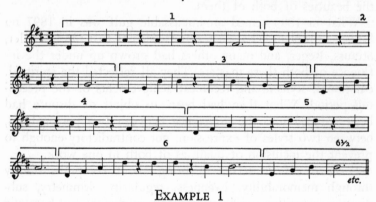

EXAMPLE 1

Here are six repetitions, and almost all are based on the alternation of tonic and dominant.

Though richer in harmony, the example from Verdi's *Il Trovatore* is of no higher order:

[54]

EXAMPLE 2

An artist or an author need not be aware that he accommodates his style to the listener's capacity of comprehension. An artist need not think very much, if only he thinks correctly and straightforwardly. He feels that he obeys the urge of a spring within himself, the urge to express himself, just like a clock, which indicates twenty-four hours every day, without questioning whether it means "this" day, this month, this year, or this century. Everyone knows this, except the clock. The artist's response to the urge of his motor occurs automatically without delay, like that of every well-lubricated mechanism.

It is obvious that one would not discuss the splitting of atoms with a person who does not know what an atom is. On the other hand, one cannot talk to a trained mind in Mother Goose fashion or in the style of what Hollywoodians call "lyrics." In the sphere of art-music, the author respects his audience. He is afraid to offend it by repeating over and over what can be understood at one single hearing, even if it is new, and let alone if it is stale old trash. A diagram may tell the whole story of a game to a chess expert; a chemist recognizes all he wants to know by glancing at a few symbols; but in a mathematical formula are combined the distant past, the actual present, and the most remote future.

Repeatedly hearing things which one likes is pleasant and need not be ridiculed. There is a subconscious desire to understand better and realize more details of the beauty. But an alert and well-trained mind will demand to be told the more remote matters, the more remote consequences of the simple matters that he has already comprehended. An alert and well-trained mind refuses to listen to baby-talk and requests strongly to be spoken to in a brief and straightforward language.

III

Progress in music consists in the development of methods of presentation which correspond to the conditions just discussed. It is the purpose of this essay to prove that Brahms, the classicist, the academician, was a great innovator in the realm of musical language, that, in fact, he was a great progressive.

This may seem contestable to an incarnate "old-Wagnerian," no matter whether he is one of the primigenial Wagnerians who has grown old, or simply an "old-Wagnerian" by birth. There were still fireproof "old-Wagnerians" born at the time of my own generation and even ten years later. Pioneers of musical progress on the one hand, and keepers of the Holy Grail of true art on the other, they considered themselves entitled to look with contempt at Brahms the classicist, the academician.

Gustav Mahler and Richard Strauss had been the first to clarify these concepts. They had both been educated in the traditional as well as in the progressive, in the Brahmsian as well as in the Wagnerian philosophy of art (*Weltanschauung*). Their example helped us to realize that there was as much organizational order, if not pedantry in Wagner as there was daring courage, if not even bizarre fantasy in Brahms. Does not the mystic correspondence of the numbers of their dates suggest some mysterious relationship between them? Brahms' one-hundredth birthday anniversary in 1933 was the fiftieth anniversary of the death of Wagner. And now, as this essay is being rewritten, we commemorate the fiftieth anniversary of Brahms' death.

Mysteries conceal a truth, but direct curiosity to unveil it.

IV

How great an innovator Brahms was in respect to harmony can be seen in this example from his string quartet in C minor, Op. 51, No. 1. (ms. 11-23).

EXAMPLE 3

This is the contrasting middle section of a ternary form whose a-section is already rich enough harmonically in comparison with the I-V or I-IV-V harmony, intermixed occasionally with a VI or III and sometimes a neapolitan triad, of Brahms' predecessors. To base a main theme on such a rich harmony seemed a daring enterprise to the ears of the time.

But the harmony of this middle section competes successfully with that of many a Wagnerian passage. Even the most progressive composers after Brahms were carefully avoiding remote deviation from the tonic region in the beginning of a piece. But this modulation to the dominant of a minor region on B, and the sudden, unceremonious and precipitate return to the tonic, is a rare case. The successsion of three major triads on E flat, D flat and C respectively in the coda of the first movement of the *Eroica* (ms. 551-561) and the juxtaposition of two unrelated triads (on B and B*b*) in the following example from Schubert are cases of a similar procedure.

EXAMPLE 4 (From Schubert's Lied: *In der Ferne*)

Examples from Wagner in which similar progressions occur are often not easily analyzed, but then prove less complicated than one might have expected. For instance, the motive of the *Todestrank*, from *Tristan und Isolde,*

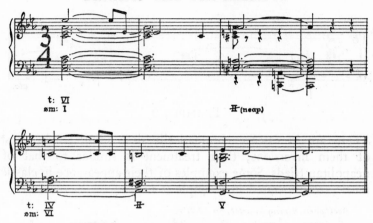

EXAMPLE 5

unmasks itself as remaining within the closer relations of the
tonality. Also not very distant is the harmonic deviation in
Isolde's order to Tristan: "Befehlen liess dem Eigenholde..."

EXAMPLE 6

But the "Traurige Weise", the English Horn solo of Act III,

EXAMPLE 7

shows in its modulatory section no more remote modulation
than the end of the a-section of the aforementioned C minor
string quartet of Brahms:

EXAMPLE 8

These are in essence chromatically descending triads, most of them inversions; their treatment is similar to that of neapolitan triads. Some examples of their appearance in classic music are illustrated in Example 9 a, b, c.

EXAMPLE 9 A, B, C

If there is no decisive difference between Brahms and Wagner as regards extension of the relationship within a tonality, it must not be overlooked that Wagner's harmony is richer in substitute harmonies and vagrants, and in a freer use of dissonances, especially of unprepared ones. On the other hand, in strophic, songlike forms and other structures, such as represent the Wagnerian version of arias, the harmony moves rather less expansively and more slowly than in similar forms of Brahms. Compare, for instance, the "Winterstürme wichen dem Wonnemond," the "Als zullendes Kind, zog ich dich auf" or the song of the Rhine Daughters to Brahms' song "Meine Liebe ist grün," or the main theme of the String Quintet in G, Op. 111, which starts roving in its third measure, or the Rhapsody, Op. 79, No. 2, which almost avoids establishing a tonality.

V

Ternary, rondo, and other rounded forms appear in dramatic music only occasionally, as episodes, mostly at lyrical resting-points where the action stops or at least slows down—in places where a composer can proceed along formal concepts and can repeat and develop without the pressure of the progress of an action, without being forced to mirror moods or events not included in the character of his material.

Dramatic music resembles in its modulatory character the modulatory elaboration (*Durchführung*) of a symphony, sonata, or other rounded form. Wagner's "Leitmotives" usually contain some germinating harmonies in which the urge for modulatory changes is inherent. But simultaneously they fulfill another task, an organizational task, which shows the formalistic side of Wagner's genius.

The recitative in pre-Wagnerian operas was also modulatory. But it was unorganized, if not incoherent, with respect to thematic and even motive requirements. The "Leitmotiv" technique represents the grandiose intention of unification of the thematic material of an entire opera, and even of an entire tetralogy. An organization as far-reaching as this deserves an aesthetic rating of the highest order. But if foresight in organization is called formalistic in the case of Brahms, then this organization is also formalistic, because it stems from the same state of mind, from one which conceives an entire work in one single creative moment and acts correspondingly.

When Brahms, towards the end of the last movement of his Fourth Symphony, carries out some of the variations by a succession of thirds,

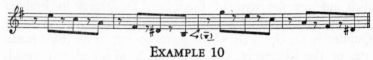

EXAMPLE 10

he unveils the relationship of the theme of the Passacaglia to the first movement. Transposed a fifth up,

EXAMPLE 11

it is identical with the first eight notes of the main theme,

EXAMPLE 12

and the theme of the passacaglia in its first half admits the contrapuntal combination with the descending thirds.

EXAMPLE 13

People generally do not know that luck is a heavenly gift, equivalent to, and of the same kind as, talent, beauty, strength, etc. It is not given for nothing—on the contrary, one must deserve it. Skeptics might attempt belittling this as a mere "lucky chance." Such people have a wrong evaluation of both luck and inspiration and are not capable of imagining what both can achieve.

It would look like a high accomplishment of intellectual gymnastics if all this had been "constructed" prior to inspired composing. But men who know the power of inspiration, and how it can produce combinations no one can foresee, also know that Wagner's application of the Leitmotiv was, in the great majority of cases, of an inspired spontaneity. As often as Siegfried came to his mind, his mind's eye and ear saw and heard him just as his motive depicts him:

(and a little later)

EXAMPLE 14 A, B, C

VI

I assume that I have been the first to lay down a principle which, about four decades ago, began directing and regulating my musical thinking and the formulation of my ideas, and which played a decisive role in my self-criticism.

I wish to join ideas with ideas. No matter what the purpose or meaning of an idea in the aggregate may be, no matter whether its function be introductory, establishing, varying, preparing, elaborating, deviating, developing, concluding, subdividing, subordinate, or basic, it must be an idea which had to take this place even if it were not to serve for this purpose or meaning or function; and this idea must look in construction and in thematic content as if it were not there to fulfill a structural task. In other words, a transition, a codetta, an elaboration, etc., should not be considered as a thing in its own end. It should not appear at all if it does not develop, modify, intensify, clarify, or throw light or color on the idea of the piece.

This does not mean that functions of these types can be absent in a composition. But it means that no space should be devoted to mere formal purposes. And it means that those segments or sections which fulfill structural requirements should do so without being mere trash.

This is no critique of classic music—it merely presents my personal artistic code of honor which everybody else may disregard. But it seems to me that the progress in which Brahms was operative should have stimulated composers to write music for adults. Mature people think in complexes, and the higher their intelligence the greater is the number of units with which they are familiar. It is inconceivable that composers should call "serious music" what they write in an obsolete style, with a prolixity not conforming to the contents—repeating three to seven times what is understandable at once. Why should it not be possible in music to say in whole complexes in a condensed form what, in the preceding epochs, had at first to be said several times with slight variations before it could be elaborated? Is it not as if a writer who wanted to tell of "somebody who lives in a house near the river" should have to explain what a house is, what it is made for, and of what material, and, after that, explain the river in the same way?

Some people speak of the "dying romanticism" of music. Do they really believe that making music, playing with tones, is something realistic, or what? Or is it that romanticism has to resign in favor of senseless prolixity?

VII

In order to grasp thoroughly the development of musical construction during the epoch from Bach to Brahms it is necessary to go back to the period when the style of contrapuntal construction was abandoned and the aesthetic of the homophonic-melodic style was formulated. Comparing the compositions manufactured in response to this aesthetic with those of J. S. Bach on the one hand and of Haydn, Mozart, Beethoven and Schubert on the other, one understands why such ruthless propaganda had to be applied to eliminate J. S. Bach, but one is astonished that such fruits can be derived from so scanty a soil.

Under the leadership of Keyser, Telemann and Mattheson, composers were asked to let alone "great art"; to strive with effort to write light (that is effortless) music; to see that a theme is provided with "a certain something" (*ein gewisses Etwas*) which seems to be familiar to everybody; to write in the light manner of the French. To Mattheson, counterpoint was a mere mental exercise without emotional power. As it has happened frequently, these men were highly estimated in their lifetime, while Bach was little known. But one must doubt that men were inspired geniuses who composed according to such advice, like cooks obeying a cookbook, or some of their music would have survived. This was not a natural development; it was not evolution, but man-made revolution. One can only express what one possesses inwardly. A style cannot make one richer. Thus these musicians live only because of the musicologists' interest in dead, decayed matter.

It is known that Mozart and Beethoven looked on some of their predecessors with great admiration. Fortunately, however, the versatility, inventiveness and power of emotion kept these masters free from the shackles of an aesthetic of popular complaisance.

VIII

True, much of the organization of classic music reveals, by its regularity, symmetry and simple harmony, its relation with, if not derivation from, popular and dance music. Construction by phrases of the same length, especially if their number of measures is two, four or eight times two, and if subdivision into two equally long segments adds a certain kind of symmetry, contributes much to memorability; knowing the first half, it is almost possible to conjecture the second half. Deviation from regularity and symmetry does not necessarily endanger comprehensibility. One might accordingly wonder why in Haydn's and Mozart's forms irregularity is more frequently present than in Beethoven's. Is it perhaps that formal finesses have diverted a listener's attention, which should concentrate upon the tremendous power of emotional expression? There are not too many cases like that of the String Quartet Op. 95 in F minor (see Example 9b).

Construction by phrases of unequal length accounts for many of the irregularities in Haydn's and Mozart's music. These differences are produced by extension of a segment, by internal repetitions or by reductions and condensations. Such is the case in many of Haydn's and Mozart's Menuets, according to which one might be inclined to consider menuets as a song-like form, rather than as a derivative of dance music.

Example 15, from a piano Sonata by Haydn, consists of two segments of two measures and two of three measures: 2 + 3 and 2 + 3.

EXAMPLE 15

Example 16 from the String Quartet in B♭ major by Mozart is richer in organization: 3+1+1+3 (the latter is perhaps a unit of 2+1).

EXAMPLE 16

The whole theme comprises eight measures; thus the irregularity is, so to speak, subcutane (i. e. it does not show up on the surface).

While Haydn's example is still symmetrical, this is entirely unsymmetrical and thereby renounces one of the most efficient aids to comprehension. But it is not yet what deserves to be called "musical prose." One might rather be inclined to ascribe such irregularity to a baroque sense of form, that is, to a desire to combine unequal, if not heterogeneous, elements into a formal unit. Though such a hypothesis is not without foundation, it seems that there is another, more artistic and psychological explanation.

Mozart has to be considered above all as a dramatic composer.

Accommodation of the music to every change of mood and action, materially or psychologically, is the most essential problem an opera composer has to master. Inability in this respect might produce incoherence—or worse, boredom. The technique of the recitative escapes this danger by avoiding motival and harmonic obligations and their consequences. The "Arioso" liquidates rapidly and ruthlessly that minimum of obligations in which it might have engaged. But the "Finales" and many "Ensembles" and even "Arias" contain heterogeneous elements to which the technique of lyric condensation is not applicable. In pieces of this type a composer must be capable of turning within the smallest space. Mozart, anticipating this necessity, begins such a piece with a melody consisting of a number of phrases of various lengths and characters, each of them pertaining to a different phase of the action and the mood. They are, in their first formulation, loosely joined together, and often simply juxtaposed, thus admitting to be broken asunder and used independently as motival material for small formal segments.

A striking example of this procedure can be seen in the Finale (No. 15) of Act 2 of *The Marriage of Figaro*. The third section of this Finale, an Allegro, starts after Susanna's line "Guardate, guardate quia scoso sarà" with a theme in B flat, consisting of the three phrases *a, b, c* in Example 17.

EXAMPLE 17 A, B, C

To this are added later *d* in ms. 22-23 and *e* in ms. 25-29.

EXAMPLE 18 D, E

This Allegro-section comprises 160 measures and contains an astonishingly great number of segments, all of which are built, almost exclusively, out of variations of these five little phrases in a constantly changing order.

Similar construction can be found in many of the ensembles, of which the Terzet (No. 7) and the Sextet (No. 18) are outstanding specimens. But even duets, though one might expect here not so loose a formulation, derive all of it from illustrating segments, whose features show little external relationship. It is admirable how closely the action and the mood of the actors is portrayed in the opening Duet (No. 1). Both Figaro and Susanna are deeply concerned about affairs of their own. Figaro is measuring the walls of their future apartment, Susanna trying on a new hat, admiring her looks—neither of them has an ear or an eye for the other person. Thus, while Figaro lays out his measuring tape (Ex. 19, phrase *a*), extends it (phrase *b*, the syncopation in the bass), and counts the number of lengths ("cinque," phrase *c*.)

[69]

EXAMPLE 19

Susanna tries in vain to attract his interest to her attire.

EXAMPLE 20

Wagner or Strauss could not do this better.

Organization based on different and differently shaped elements proves to be a vision of the future. A composer of operas, of oratorios (as Schweitzer shows in analyzing Bach's music to words) or even of songs, who does not prepare for far remote necessities acts as silly and brainless as a pedantic performer who insists on playing classic music with metronomically measured equal beats—as if it were dance music. Of course, in the stiff confinement of a Procrustean bed, no modification can fit, and even those ritardandi and accelerandi (Schumann's "immer schneller werdend") which the composer himself demands will never turn out satisfactorily.

A wise performer, one who is indeed a "servant to the work," one who possesses the mental elasticity of a rank equal to that of a musical thinker—such a man will proceed like Mozart or Schubert or others. He will systematize irregularity, making it a component principle of the organization.

IX

Analysts of my music will have to realize how much I personally owe to Mozart. People who looked unbelievingly at me, thinking I made a poor joke, will now understand why I called myself a "pupil of Mozart," must now understand my reasons. This will not help them to appreciate my music, but to understand Mozart. And it will teach young composers what are the essentials that one has to learn from masters and the way one can apply these lessons without loss of personality.

Mozart himself had learned from Italian and French composers. He had probably learned also from Ph. E. Bach. But certainly it was his own musical thinking that enabled him to produce constructions like the abovementioned ones.

The preceding analysis may have suggested the idea that irregular and unsymmetrical construction is an absolute and inescapable result of dramatic composing. If this were true one ought to find more of it in Wagner's music. However, Wagner, who in his first period was strongly influenced by contemporary Italians, has seldom abandoned a two-by-two-measure construction, but has made great progress in the direction of musical prose—that is, toward the goal which Brahms also strove for, but on a different road. The difference between these two men is not what their contemporaries thought; it is not the difference between Dionysian and Apollonian art, as Nietzsche might have called it. Besides, it is not as simple as that between Dionysius and Apollo: that the one, in intoxication, smashes the glasses which the other has produced in an intoxication of imagination. Things happen thus only (if this is not too pompous a word for what is so little and so late) in the imagination of a biographer or a musicologist. Intoxication, whether Dionysian or Apollonian, of an artist's fantasy increases the clarity of his vision.

Great art must proceed to precision and brevity. It presupposes the alert mind of an educated listener who, in a single act of thinking, includes with every concept all associations pertaining to the complex. This enables a musician to write for upper-class minds, not only doing what grammar and idiom require, but, in other respects lending to every sentence the full pregnancy of meaning of a maxim, of a proverb, of an aphorism. This is what musical prose should be—a direct and straightforward presentation of ideas, without any patchwork, without mere padding and empty repetitions.

Density of texture is certainly an obstacle to popularity; but prolixity alone cannot guarantee general favor. Real popularity, lasting popularity, is only attained in those rare cases where power of expression is granted to men who dwell intensely in the sphere of basic human sentiments. There are a few cases in Schubert and Verdi, but many in Johann Strauss. Even Mozart, when, in the *Magic Flute,* he temporarily abandoned his own highly refined and artistic style of presentation in favor of the semi-popular characters he had to portray musically, did not fully succeed; the popular parts of this opera never attained the success of the serious parts. His stand was on the side of Sarastro and his priests.

In the epoch between Mozart and Wagner one does not find many themes of an irregular construction. But the following example, a transition from the end of the main theme to the subordinate theme in the first movement of Mozart's String Quartet in D minor, certainly deserves the qualification of musical prose.

EXAMPLE 21

Even if one ignores the first four little phrases which conclude the main theme, and also the imitations (marked 14th
and 17th) by which the modulation is finished, there remain
nine little phrases varying in size and character within no more
than eight measures. The smallest (the 5th, 6th and 7th) are
only three eighth notes long—in spite of which they are so
expressive that one is almost tempted to put words under-
neath. One regrets not possessing the power of a poet to render
in words what these phrases tell. However, poetry and lyrics
would not deprive it of the quality of being prose-like in the
unexcelled freedom of its rhythm and the perfect independence
from formal symmetry.

[73]

Asymmetry, combinations of phrases of differing lengths, numbers of measures not divisible by eight, four or even two, i.e. imparity of the number of measures, and other irregularities already appear in the earliest works of Brahms. The main theme of the first Sextet in B flat, Op. 18, consists of nine measures (or, rather, ten, because of the upbeat-like measure which introduces the repetition of this theme in the first violin at*).

EXAMPLE 22

The construction then appears as 3 (or 1+2)+2+2+2+1=10.

The subordinate theme of the same movement connects its two motive forms a and b, first to build two two-measure phrases followed by a three-measure and a two-measure phrase, totaling nine measures.

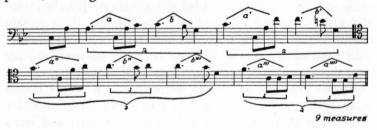

EXAMPLE 23

The Scherzo from the second Sextet, Op. 36, starts with a theme which comprises seventeen measures, though in the seventeenth measure another phrase begins overlappingly.

EXAMPLE 24

There are two rhythmical shifts (at *), but the most interesting feature is presented by the ambiguity of the ending of the second phrase. One wonders whether measures 9ff. do not belong to this phrase.

Though these irregularities do not measure up to the artfulness of the Mozart examples, they still present a more advanced phase of the development toward liberation from formal restrictions of musical thoughts, because they do not derive from a baroque feeling, or from necessities of illustration, as is the case in dramatic music.

Other asymmetrical structures occur in songs of Brahms. They derive probably in part from the rhythmic peculiarities of the poems upon which they are based. It is well known that Brahms' aesthetic canon demanded that the melody of a song must reflect, in one way or another, the number of metrical feet in the poem. Accordingly, if there were three, four, or five metrical feet, the melody should consist of the same number of measures or half-measures. For instance, the first half of "Meerfahrt" (H. Heine) consists exclusively of three-measure phrases, on account of the poem's meter of three metrical feet.

> Mein Líebchen wir sássen beisámmen
> tráulich im léichten Káhn

EXAMPLE 25

The *Lied* "Feldeinsamkeit" is based on verses of five metrical feet; accordingly, one might expect that the corresponding first two phrases would be five measures of five half-measures long. But the first phrase is condensed to two measures, to which the second phrase adds three measures, thus reflecting the meter of the verses.

EXAMPLE 26

The poem "Am Sonntag Morgen zierlich angetan" has *five* metrical feet, but the melody consists of phrases three measures long, that is, six half-measures—the result of the prolongation of the pause between the phrases, which could be a sixteenth-rest only.

EXAMPLE 27

Geuss nícht so láut der líebentflammten Líeder
Tónréichen Scháll
Vom Blútenást des Ápfelbáums h	erníeder
Ó Náchtigáll

This poem has an interesting meter: 5+3+5+3 metrical feet.
Note also the spondaic meter of every second line. The dotted
half note in measure 2 causes the extension of the first phrase
to six, or rather seven half-measures. The second line, if treated
proportionally, should comprise about four half-measures, but
occupies, inclusive of the half-rest, five half-measures.

EXAMPLE 28

These irregularities are more than the meter of the poem
demands. In many other examples the length of the phrase
differs from the number of metrical feet; for instance, in
Example 29, the two times three metrical feet of the first
two lines could fit well in the space of seven or eight half-
measures, instead of the seventeen half-measures apportioned
to them.

EXAMPLE 29

Similarly, the poem "An den Mond," with its regular
rhythm of four metrical feet, does not require the three-
measure construction.

EXAMPLE 30

"Beim Abschied" has lines of four rhythmical feet, but the phrases are stretched to occupy five measures.

EXAMPLE 31

The irregularity is also not required by the meter (four metrical feet) of the poem in "Mädchenlied." It is the inserted fifth measure, the stretching in measures 8 and 9 and the addition of two one-measure phrases that bring up to ten and twelve measures respectively what could be put into eight measures.

EXAMPLE 32

The irregularities of "Immer leiser wird mein Schlummer" are partly caused by the changing meter of the poem.

EXAMPLE 33

But an attempt to condense these phrases

EXAMPLE 34

illustrates at once that the little piano interludes which separate and prolong the phrases are suggested by the mood of the poem. This looser construction prepares for an even richer freedom of phrasing which occurs in this continuation.

The same foresight may be the cause of the extensions in "Verrat" (Example 35). There is no metrical feature demanding the fifth and the tenth measures, both of which are again piano interludes. In later parts of the poem deviations from this meter occur, and this is the place where deviations from even-numbered structures increase. In Example 35b a few cases are illustrated. The length of the phrases is different, and the upbeats with which they begin (marked ⋏) fluctuate between one, three, and five eighths.

EXAMPLE 35

The most important capacity of a composer is to cast a glance into the most remote future of his themes or motives. He has to be able to know beforehand the consequences which derive from the problems existing in his material, and to organize everything accordingly. Whether he does this consciously or subconsciously is a subordinate matter. It suffices if the result proves it.

Thus one must not be astonished by an act of genius when a composer, feeling that irregularity will occur later, already deviates in the beginning from simple regularity. An unprepared and sudden change of structural principles would endanger balance.

XI

I cannot renounce the opportunity to illustrate the remoteness of a genius' foresight. In Example 36a (Beethoven's String Quartet Op. 95) there appear in the first measure the three notes D*b*, C♮ and D♮ (36a and b).

EXAMPLE 36 A-G

In Example 36c this succession is retrograded to D♮, C♮, D♭ and transposed a seventh up.

A comparison of Example 37a, b, and c with Example 36d, e, f, and g unveils the origin of the enigmatic procedures in the upper and lower voices of measures 7-9 and simultaneously shows how the strange figure in measure 36 (example 37b) is related to the basic idea.

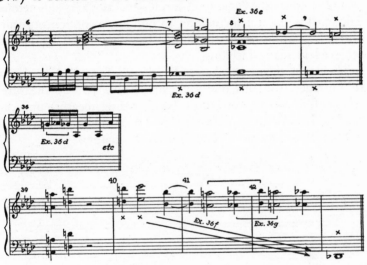

EXAMPLE 37 A, B, C

Moreover, the relation of the still more enigmatic segment in measures 38-43 (and later in 49-54) with the main theme is thus revealed. The same succession of tones, direct and reversed, appears also several times in the following movements. It would be presumptuous to say that it is "the" basic feature of the structure, or that it had a great influence on the organization of this string quartet; perhaps its function is only that of a "connective." I believe its reappearances, its reincarnation in other themes can just as well be caused subconsciously; the mind of a composer is dominated by every detail of his idea, the consequences of which accordingly will show up involuntarily and unexpectedly. Of course, only a master who is sure of himself, of his sense of form and balance, can renounce conscious control in favor of the dictates of his imagination.

XII

Illustrations of the tendency toward asymmetrical construction among post-Wagnerian composers are very numerous. Though the natural inclination to build two- or four-measure phrases is still present, deviation from multiples of two is achieved in many fashions.

The main theme of Anton Bruckner's Seventh Symphony, for instance, contains one segment of five (3+2) measures and another of three measures. Neither three-measure unit can be classified as an extension of two measures or a condensation of four measures. They are both "natural."

See also 8th.

EXAMPLE 38

The asymmetry in the main theme of Gustav Mahler's Second Symphony is due to the irregular appearance of one-measure units.

EXAMPLE 39

The irregularities in the subordinate theme of the Scherzo in Mahler's Sixth Symphony are only partly caused by its composition of 3/8, 4/8, and 3/4 meter. The units are also different in length. The first two comprise seven eighth notes, the third comprises ten eighth notes and in the continuation even greater differences appear. Also these irregularities could scarcely be traced back to even numbers.

EXAMPLE 40

An extraordinary case, even among contemporary composers, is the melody from "Abschied," the last movement of Mahler's *Lied von der Erde*. All the units vary greatly in shape, size and content, as if they were not motival parts of a melodic unit, but words, each of which has a purpose of its own in the sentence.

EXAMPLE 41

The main theme from Richard Strauss' *Symphonia Domestica* is distinctly an indivisible unit of five measures. It ends overlapping the entrance of the oboe.

EXAMPLE 42

Another theme of the same work consists of two- and one-measure units.

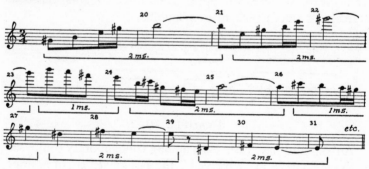

EXAMPLE 43

Also, an indivisible five-measure unit is the first phrase of Max Reger's Violin Concerto. A three-measure phrase completes this part of the sentence.

[84]

EXAMPLE 44

The 'cello solo from "Serenade" (Schoenberg, *Pierrot Lunaire*, Op. 21) consists of an irregular change of one- and two-measure units.

EXAMPLE 45

XIII

One might interpret some of the irregularities in the examples from Haydn, Mozart and Brahms as caused by special purposes, as, for instance, the desire to satisfy a baroque sense of form; or to accomplish a more definite separation of the phrases by "punctuation;" or to assist in the dramatic characterization of various actors in an opera; or to comply with the metrical peculiarities of the poem of a song—as has been shown in previous discussions.

But none of these reasons will explain irregularities such as have been mentioned in the music of post-Wagnerian composers. Evidently their deviations from simple construction no longer derive from exclusively technical conditions, nor do they serve to provide a stylistic appearance. They have become incorporated into the syntax and grammar of perhaps all subsequent musical structures. Accordingly, they have ceased to be recorded as merits of a composition—though unfortunately many illiterate composers still write two plus two, four plus four, eight plus eight unchangingly.

XIV

Again: it does not matter whether an artist attains his highest achievements consciously, according to a preconceived plan, or subconsciously, by stepping blindfolded from one feature to the next. Has the Lord granted to a thinker a brain of unusual power? Or did the Lord silently assist him now and then with a bit of His own thinking? Our Lord is an extremely good chess player. He usually plans billions of moves ahead, and that is why it is not easy to understand Him. It seems, however, that He likes helping in their spiritual problems those He has selected—though not enough in their more material ones.

Again: asymmetry and imparity of structural elements are no miracle in contemporary music, nor do they constitute a merit. A contemporary composer connects phrases irrespective of their size and shape, only vigilant of harmonic progression, of rhythmic and motival contents, fluency and logic. But otherwise he chooses his way like a tourist, freely and nonchalantly if he feels he has time, strictly and carefully if he feels he is under pressure. If only he never loses sight of his goal!

Merits of contemporary compositions may consist of formal finesses of a different kind. It may be the variety and multitude of the ideas, the manner in which they develop and grow out of germinating units, how they are contrasted and how they complement one another; it may also be their emotional quality, romantic or unromantic, subjective or objective, their expression of moods and characters and illustration.

Contemporary compositorial technique has not yet arrived at a freedom of construction comparable to that of a language. Evidently, however, parity and symmetry play a lesser role today than they did in earlier techniques; and the aspiration for a strictness resembling that of the hexameter or pentameter, or that of the structures of the sonnet or the stanza in poetry is rare. There are even composers who preserve little of the features of the theme in their variations—a queer case: why should one use a form of such strictness, if one aims for the contrary? Is it not as if one would string a violin E-string on a double bass? One is ready to ignore discrepancies of this kind and degree in favor of overwhelming merits in other respects. But the esthetic background for a just and general judgment has become very questionable at present.

XV

This discussion will be concluded by two illustrations of Brahms' contribution toward the development of the musical language: the main theme of the Andante from the A minor String Quartet, Op. 51, No. 2, and the third of the "Vier Ernste Gesänge," Op. 121, "O Tod, O Tod, wie bitter bist du!".

Both these themes are specimens of a perhaps unique artistic quality, as regards their motival elaboration and internal organization.

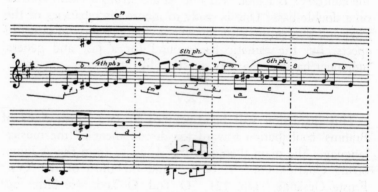

EXAMPLE 46

As the analysis unveils, the A major Andante contains exclusively motive forms which can be explained as derivatives of the interval of a second, marked by brackets *a*:

b then is the inversion upward of *a*;

c is *a+b*;

d is part of *c*;

e is *b+b*, descending seconds, comprising a fourth;

f is the interval of a fourth, abstracted from *e*, in inversion.

The first phrase—*c*—thus consists of *a* plus *b*. It also contains *d* (see bracket below), which also functions as a connective between the first and the second phrase (at *).

The second phrase consists of *e* and *d*; with the exception of its upbeat (the eighth note e) and the two notes c# and b, it presents itself as a transposition of the first phrase (see above at #), one step higher. It also furnishes the interval of a fourth, *f*.

The third phrase contains *e* twice, the second time transposed one step higher.

The fourth phrase is distinctly a transformed transposition of *c*.

The fifth phrase, though it looks like a variant of the preceding phrase, merely contains *c*, connected with the preceding by *f*.

The sixth phrase, consisting of *e, d,* and *b,* contains a chromatic connective b#, which could be considered as the second note of a form of *a*. This b# is the only note in the whole theme whose derivation can be contested.

Skeptics, however, might reason that steps of a second or even fractions of a scale are present in every theme without constituting the thematic material. There exists an enormous multitude of methods and principles of construction, few of which have yet been explored. I deem it probable that many musicians are acquainted with these two analyses which I broadcast in 1933 on celebrating Brahms' 100th birthday anniversary. But one who objects to my conclusions must not forget that the second example exhibits a similar secret, this time dealing with thirds.

EXAMPLE 47

This example has a certain resemblance to the main theme of Brahms' Fourth Symphony—in both the structural unit is the interval of a third. The first phrase in the voice part consists of a succession of three thirds b - g, g - e and e - c, marked *a*.

[90]

The second phrase is built from the inversion of *a*, c# - e, marked *b*, and *c*, which is *a* with an inserted passing note c.

The third phrase is a sequence of the second phrase and is (characteristically!) a third lower.

The fourth phrase, in which the voice follows the piano with a small canonic imitation, inverts the interval of a third (b - g and e - c respectively) into a sixth *d*. Observe also the relation of a third between the two points * - * in measures 6 - 7 in voice and piano.

The fifth and sixth phrases, with part of the seventh, are founded upon the notes marked *f*, g - b - d - f#, which are an inversion of the three descending thirds of the first phrase. Besides, the left hand in measures 8 and 9 contains the succession of thirds, though the first two notes have changed their places (see **). Furthermore, the left hand in measure 10 contains six tones building a chain of thirds *e*. The voice part consists mainly of thirds, some of them including passing notes. Besides, here where the climactic concentration approaches a cadence, the interval of a third appears abundantly, and *e* also occurs in successions.

See also Example 48a and b. Here again the third is reversed as a sixth (48a) in the voice and imitated in the bass (48b).

EXAMPLE 48 A and B

The sense of logic and economy and the power of inventiveness which build melodies of so much natural fluency deserve the admiration of every music lover who expects more than sweetness and beauty from music. But though I know offhand only one example of such complexity of construction by a pre-Brahmsian composer—by Mozart, of course (see Example 50 from the Piano Quartet in G minor)—I must state that structural analysis reveals even greater merits.

The Andante from the A minor String Quartet (Example 46) contains six phrases in eight measures. The length of these phrases is 6+6+6+ 4+4+6 quarter notes. The first three phrases occupy five and three-eighths (or five and one-half) measures. The first phrase ends practically on the first beat of measure 2. In order to appreciate fully the artistic value of the second phrase's metrical shift, one must realize that even some of the great composers, Brahms' predecessors, might have continued as in Example 49, placing the second phrase in the third measure.

EXAMPLE 49

Brahms might have tried to place the first three phrases into three 6/4 measures.

EXAMPLE 50

If, then, the next two phrases would fit into two 4/4 measures, it might be doubtful whether the accentuation of the last phrase (at *) is adequate, if all the preceding phrases had their main accents placed on first beats. But, besides, this notation would reveal the imparity of the construction even more, because the theme then becomes seven measures.

In Brahms' notation these subcutane beauties are accommodated within eight measures; and if eight measures constitute an aesthetic principle, it is preserved here in spite of the great freedom of construction.

The example from Mozart (Example 51) is an enigma—
not to the performer, but to the analyst who is interested in
the grammar, syntax, and linguistics of music.

EXAMPLE 51 A-E

It consists of three little segments, or phrases, whose metrical position is intricate. The beginning of the first phrase on a
third beat is marked *sf*, demanding a stronger accent than the
third beat usually carries. The following first beat is marked

p and if this means "cancellation of the accent,"[2] one might assume that it means a change of time, as indicated in Example 51d and 51e, where the changes of the meter are carried out. But in measure 2, the fourth beat is also marked *sf* and accentuation of the following beat is also cancelled, or at least reduced. For this reason one might suppose that the second phrase does not begin, as the brackets above indicate, at the second beat of measure 3, but at the fourth beat of measure 2, with the *sf,* as indicated below the left hand. It is also possible that the note on the third beat (the f♯) should retain its accent, thus producing a spondee.

In addition to all these problems, the 'cello, when this little segment is repeated, contributes a problem of its own, by *sf*-accents which partly contradict those of the main voice (Example 51b). The structural intricacy of this example is paralleled by the polyrhythmic construction of the second variation in the Finale of the String Quartet in D minor (Example 52a). Today one will write this as in Example 52b. In Example 51c, an example from the Menuet of the C major String Quartet may serve as a further justification for entering into an examination of such subtle problems. Example 52c is one which suggests a phrasing contrary to the meter. Here a unit of five quarter-notes is repeated on different beats, while the accompaniment remains unchanged.

---

[2] I use in my music for similar purposes the symbols / and ᴗ, borrowed from prosody. Thus changes of accentuation and rhythmic shifts are indicated. See Example 51 c.

EXAMPLE 52

Beethoven is a great innovator as regards rhythm. Remember, for instance, the last movement of the Piano Concerto in Eb, or the Menuet of the String Quartet, Op. 18 No. 6, etc. But structurally, as previously stated, he is generally rather simple. Though, however, the lucidity of presentation balances satisfactorily the heavy load of emotions his ideas carry with them, it is needless to say that abandonment of Mozart's unequal and unsymmetric foundations would have been an extremely regrettable loss. The idea cannot be rejected that the mental pleasure caused by structural beauty can be tantamount to the pleasure deriving from emotional qualities. In this sense Brahms' merit would be immense, even if he had preserved this way of thinking only in the manner of a technical device. But—and this characterizes his high rank—he has surpassed it.

If a man who knows that he will die soon makes his account with earth and with heaven, prepares his soul for the departure, and balances what he leaves with what he will receive, he might desire to incorporate a word—a part of the wisdom he has acquired—into the knowledge of mankind, if he is one of the Great. One might doubt about the sense of life if it then would be a mere accident that such a work, a life-terminating work, would not represent more than just another opus. Or is one entitled to assume that a message from a man who is already half on the other side progresses to the uttermost limit of the still-expressible? Is one not entitled to expect therefrom perfection of an extraordinary degree, because mastership, a heavenly gift, which cannot be acquired by the most painstaking assiduity and exercise, manifests itself only once, only one single time in its full entirety, when a message of such importance has to be formulated?

I imagine that at this point Brahms' protective wall of dryness might enter the picture, and that he might stop me: "Now it's enough poetry. If you have to say something, say it briefly and technically without so much sentimental fuss."

Before obeying this order, I am pressed to say that this third of the *Vier Ernste Gesänge,* "O Tod, O Tod, wie bitter bist du," seems to me the most touching of the whole cycle—in spite of its perfection, if not *because* of it. Intuition, inspiration and spontaneity in creation are generally characteristically combined with speed. But "was glaubt er, dass ich an seine elende Geige denke, wenn der Geist mich packt?" (Do you really suppose I think of your miserable violin, if the spirit gets hold of me?)—this is how the artist himself feels whether he creates in hard labor or only by a kind of toying.

There is no doubt that Brahms believed in working out the ideas which he called "gifts of grace." Hard labor is, to a trained mind, no torture, but rather a pleasure. As I have stated on another occasion: if a mathematician's or a chess player's mind can perform such miracles of the brain, why should a musician's mind not be able to do it? After all, an improviser must anticipate before playing, and composing is a slowed-down improvisation; often one cannot write fast enough to keep up with the stream of ideas. But a craftsman likes to be conscious of what he produces; he is proud of the ability of his hands, of the flexibility of his mind, of his subtle sense of balance, of his never-failing logic, of the multitude of variations, and last but not least of the profundity of his idea and his capacity of penetrating to the most remote consequences of an idea. One cannot do this with a shallow idea, but one can, and one can *only*, with a profound idea—and there one *must*.

It is important to realize that at a time when all believed in "expression," Brahms, without renouncing beauty and emotion, proved to be a progressive in a field which had not been cultivated for half a century. He would have been a pioneer if he had simply returned to Mozart. But he did not live on inherited fortune; he made one of his own. True, Wagner has contributed to the development of structural formulations through his technique of repetitions, varied or unvaried, because they freed him from the obligation of elaborating longer than necessary upon subjects which he had already clearly determined. Thus this language admitted turning to other subjects, when the action on the stage demanded it.

Brahms never wrote dramatic music—and it was rumored in Vienna that he had said he would rather write in the style of Mozart than in the "Neudeutsche Stil." One can be sure it would not have been Mozart's style, but pure Brahms, and though he might have repeated whole sentences, and even single words of the text, in the manner of pre-Wagnerian opera, he could not have entirely disregarded the contemporary feeling for dramatic presentation; he would not let an actor die during a da capo aria, and repeat the beginning after death. On the other hand, it would be highly enlightening to see all the dramatico-musical requirements carried out over Brahms' immensely advanced harmony.

It might be doubtful whether Brahms could have found a libretto fitting to what he liked and to the emotion he was capable of expressing. Would it have been a comic opera, a comedy, a lyric drama or a tragedy? He is many-sided, and one can easily find in his music expressions of all sorts, with the possible exception of violent dramatic outbursts such as one finds in Wagner and Verdi. Who knows? If one considers Beethoven's *Fidelio,* which is distinctly symphonic in its organization, remembers the tremendous outburst at the end of the second act, "O namenlose Freude!" (Oh inexpressible joy!) and compares that with the strictly symphonic style of the greater part of the third act, one may get an impression of what a genius is capable "wenn der Geist ihn packt."

"O Tod, O Tod, wie bitter bist du" has been analyzed as regards its eminent motival logic. In Example 47 are also marked the beauties of its phrasing. It seems superfluous to discuss these features here in detail; a few remarks should suffice to illustrate what has been contended in the course of this research.

The whole first part of this song contains in twelve measures thirty-six half notes. The phrasing (in the voice) apportions six half notes to the first phrase, four to the second, five to the third, five and a half to the fourth, three and a half to the fifth (counting only one upbeat eighth-note), three to the sixth, four and a half to the seventh, and five and a half to the ending phrase. One may appreciate the rhythmic shift of the third phrase to another beat and a further shift produced through the beginning of the little canon in measures 6 and 7.

Brahms' domain as a composer of songs, chamber music and symphonies has to be qualified as epic-lyric. The freedom of his language would be less surprising were he a dramatist. His influence has already produced a further development of the musical language toward an unrestricted, though well-balanced presentation of musical ideas. But, curiously, the merits of his achievements will shine brighter when more and more are incorporated into the dramatic technique. The opera composer will then become able to renounce a makeshift technique which is a shortcoming not only in the operas of the great pre-Wagnerians. As the contribution of the singer-actor to the dramatic expression is only a part of the drama, the orchestra, at first only an accompanying factor, has developed into a dominant one. It not only illustrates mood, character and action, but also determines the tempo of the action, and, through its own formal conditions, extends or limits all that happens. In order to realize the consequences of the orchestra's predominance, one must remember the frequent repetitions of text in pre-Wagnerian operas. They serve to correspond to the trend towards expansion of the form originated in the orchestra. Then there are those occasions when a melody does not accommodate to the text. These are the places where the singer dwells on the dominant of the chord while the orchestra continues to build up the formal and thematic elaborations of his part. These are the places in more recent works where the orchestra plays like a symphony, showing little regard for the requirements of the singer, and—an ultramodern pseudo-progressive accomplishment—complete disregard for what is to be expressed by the stage, word and voice, sometimes even counteracting them.

Applying here Brahms' contributions to an unrestricted musical language will enable the opera composer to overcome the metrical handicaps of his libretto's prose; the production of melodies and other structural elements will not depend on the versification, on the meter, or on the absence of possibilities for repetitions. There will be no expansion necessary for mere formal reasons and changes of mood or character will not endanger the organization. The singer will be granted the opportunity to sing and to be heard; he will not be forced to recite on a single note, but will be offered melodic lines of interest; in a word, he will not be merely the one who pronounces the words in order to make the action understandable. He will be a singing instrument of the performance.

It seems—if this is not wishful thinking—that some progress has already been made in this direction, some progress in the direction toward an unrestricted musical language which was inaugurated by Brahms the Progressive.

Composition with Twelve Tones [1]

I

TO UNDERSTAND the very nature of creation one must acknowledge that there was no light before the Lord said: "Let there be Light." And since there was not yet light, the Lord's omniscience embraced a vision of it which only His omnipotence could call forth.

We poor human beings, when we refer to one of the better minds among us as a creator, should never forget what a creator is in reality.

A creator has a vision of something which has not existed before this vision.

And a creator has the power to bring his vision to life, the power to realize it.

In fact, the concept of creator and creation should be formed in harmony with the Divine Model; inspiration and perfection, wish and fulfillment, will and accomplishment coincide spontaneously and simultaneously. In Divine Creation there were no details to be carried out later; "There was Light" at once and in its ultimate perfection.

Alas, human creators, if they be granted a vision, must travel the long path between vision and accomplishment; a hard road where, driven out of Paradise, even geniuses must reap their harvest in the sweat of their brows.

Alas, it is one thing to envision in a creative instant of inspiration and it is another thing to materialize one's vision by painstakingly connecting details until they fuse into a kind of organism.

---

[1] Delivered as a lecture at the University of California at Los Angeles, March 26, 1941.

And alas, suppose it becomes an organism, a homunculus or a robot, and possesses some of the spontaneity of a vision; it remains yet another thing to organize this form so that it becomes a comprehensible message "to whom it may concern."

II

Form in the arts, and especially in music, aims primarily at comprehensibility. The relaxation which a satisfied listener experiences when he can follow an idea, its development, and the reasons for such development is closely related, psychologically speaking, to a feeling of beauty. Thus, artistic value demands comprehensibility, not only for intellectual, but also for emotional satisfaction. However, the creator's *idea* has to be presented, whatever the *mood* he is impelled to evoke.

Composition with twelve tones has no other aim than comprehensibility. In view of certain events in recent musical history, this might seem astonishing, for works written in this style have failed to gain understanding in spite of the new medium of organization. Thus, should one forget that contemporaries are not final judges, but are generally overruled by history, one might consider this method doomed. But, though it seems to increase the listener's difficulties, it compensates for this deficiency by penalizing the composer. For composing thus does not become easier, but rather ten times more difficult. Only the better-prepared composer can compose for the better-prepared music lover.

III

The method of composing with twelve tones grew out of a necessity.

In the last hundred years, the concept of harmony has changed tremendously through the development of chromaticism. The idea that one basic tone, the root, dominated the construction of chords and regulated their succession—the concept of *tonality*—had to develop first into the concept of *extended tonality*. Very soon it became doubtful whether such a root still remained the center to which every harmony and harmonic succession must be referred. Furthermore, it became doubtful whether a tonic appearing at the beginning, at the end, or at any other point really had a constructive meaning. Richard Wagner's harmony had promoted a change in the logic and constructive power of harmony. One of its consequences was the so-called *impressionistic* use of harmonies, especially practised by Debussy. His harmonies, without constructive meaning, often served the coloristic purpose of expressing moods and pictures. Moods and pictures, though extra-musical, thus became constructive elements, incorporated in the musical functions; they produced a sort of emotional comprehensibility. In this way, tonality was already dethroned in practise, if not in theory. This alone would perhaps not have caused a radical change in compositional technique. However, such a change became necessary when there occurred simultaneously a development which ended in what I call the *emancipation of the dissonance.*

The ear had gradually become acquainted with a great number of dissonances, and so had lost the fear of their "sense-interrupting" effect. One no longer expected preparations of Wagner's dissonances or resolutions of Strauss' discords; one was not disturbed by Debussy's non-functional harmonies, or by the harsh counterpoint of later composers. This state of affairs led to a freer use of dissonances comparable to classic composers' treatment of diminished seventh chords, which could precede and follow any other harmony, consonant or dissonant, as if there were no dissonance at all.

What distinguishes dissonances from consonances is not a greater or lesser degree of beauty, but a greater or lesser degree of *comprehensibility.* In my *Harmonielehre* I presented the theory that dissonant tones appear later among the overtones, for which reason the ear is less intimately acquainted with them. This phenomenon does not justify such sharply contradictory terms as concord and discord. Closer acquaintance with the more remote consonances—the dissonances, that is—

gradually eliminated the difficulty of comprehension and finally admitted not only the emancipation of dominant and other seventh chords, diminished sevenths and augmented triads, but also the emancipation of Wagner's, Strauss', Moussorgsky's, Debussy's, Mahler's, Puccini's, and Reger's more remote dissonances.

The term *emancipation of the dissonance* refers to its comprehensibility, which is considered equivalent to the consonance's comprehensibility. A style based on this premise treats dissonances like consonances and renounces a tonal center. By avoiding the establishment of a key modulation is excluded, since modulation means leaving an established tonality and establishing *another* tonality.

The first compositions in this new style were written by me around 1908 and, soon afterwards, by my pupils, Anton von Webern and Alban Berg. From the very beginning such compositions differed from all preceding music, not only harmonically but also melodically, thematically, and motivally. But the foremost characteristics of these pieces *in statu nascendi* were their extreme expressiveness and their extraordinary brevity. At that time, neither I nor my pupils were conscious of the reasons for these features. Later I discovered that our sense of form was right when it forced us to counterbalance extreme emotionality with extraordinary shortness. Thus, subconsciously, consequences were drawn from an innovation which, like every innovation, destroys while it produces. New colorful harmony was offered; but much was lost.

Formerly the harmony had served not only as a source of beauty, but, more important, as a means of distinguishing the features of the form. For instance, only a consonance was considered suitable for an ending. Establishing functions demanded different successions of harmonies than roving functions; a bridge, a transition, demanded other successions than a codetta; harmonic variation could be executed intelligently and logically only with due consideration of the fundamental meaning of the harmonies. Fulfillment of all these functions—comparable to the effect of punctuation in the construction of sentences, of subdivision into paragraphs, and of fusion into chapters—could scarcely be assured with chords whose constructive values had not as yet been explored. Hence, it seemed at first impossible to compose pieces of complicated organization or of great length.

A little later I discovered how to construct larger forms by following a text or a poem. The differences in size and shape of its parts and the change in character and mood were mirrored in the shape and size of the composition, in its dynamics and tempo, figuration and accentuation, instrumentation and orchestration. Thus the parts were differentiated as clearly as they had formerly been by the tonal and structural functions of harmony.

IV

Formerly the use of the fundamental harmony had been theoretically regulated through recognition of the effects of root progressions. This practise had grown into a subconsciously functioning *sense of form* which gave a real composer an almost somnambulistic sense of security in creating, with utmost precision, the most delicate distinctions of formal elements.

Whether one calls oneself conservative or revolutionary, whether one composes in a conventional or progressive manner, whether one tries to imitate old styles or is destined to express new ideas—whether one is a good composer or not—one must be convinced of the infallibility of one's own fantasy and one must believe in one's own inspiration. Nevertheless, the desire for a conscious control of the new means and forms will arise in every artist's mind; and he will wish to know *consciously* the laws and rules which govern the forms which he has conceived "as in a dream." Strongly convincing as this dream may have been, the conviction that these new sounds obey the laws of nature and of our manner of thinking—the conviction that order, logic, comprehensibility and form cannot be present without obedience to such laws—forces the composer along the road of exploration. He must find, if not laws or rules, at least ways to justify the dissonant character of these harmonies and their successions.

V

After many unsuccessful attempts during a period of approximately twelve years, I laid the foundations for a new procedure in musical construction which seemed fitted to replace those structural differentiations provided formerly by tonal harmonies.

I called this procedure *Method of Composing with Twelve Tones Which are Related Only with One Another.*

This method consists primarily of the constant and exclusive use of a set of twelve different tones. This means, of course, that no tone is repeated within the series and that it uses all twelve tones of the chromatic scale, though in a different order. It is in no way identical with the chromatic scale.[2]

EXAMPLE 1

Example 1 shows that such a basic set (BS) consists of various intervals. It should never be called a scale, although it is invented to substitute for some of the unifying and formative advantages of scale and tonality. The scale is the source of many figurations, parts of melodies and melodies

---

2 Curiously and wrongly, most people speak of the "system" of the chromatic scale. Mine is no system but only a method, which means a *modus* of applying regularly a preconceived formula. *A method can, but need not,* be one of the consequences of a system. I am also not the inventor of the chromatic scale; somebody else must have occupied himself with this task long ago.

themselves, ascending and descending passages, and even broken chords. In approximately the same manner the tones of the basic set produce similar elements. Of course, cadences produced by the distinction between principal and subsidiary harmonies will scarcely be derived from the basic set. But something different and more important is derived from it with a regularity comparable to the regularity and logic of the earlier harmony; the association of tones into harmonies and their successions is regulated (as will be shown later) by the order of these tones. The basic set functions in the manner of a motive. This explains why such a basic set has to be invented anew for every piece. It has to be the first creative thought. It does not make much difference whether or not the set appears in the composition at once like a theme or a melody, whether or not it is characterized as such by features of rhythm, phrasing, construction, character, etc.

Why such a set should consist of twelve different tones, why none of these tones should be repeated too soon, why, accordingly, only one set should be used in one composition—the answers to all these questions came to me gradually.

Discussing such problems in my *Harmonielehre* (1911), I recommended the avoidance of octave doublings.[3] To double is to emphasize, and an emphasized tone could be interpreted as a root, or even as a tonic; the consequences of such an interpretation must be avoided. Even a slight reminiscence of the former tonal harmony would be disturbing, because it would create false expectations of consequences and continuations. The use of a tonic is deceiving if it is not based on *all* the relationship of tonality.

The use of more than one set was excluded because in every following set one or more tones would have been repeated too soon. Again there would arise the danger of interpreting the repeated tone as a tonic. Besides, the effect of unity would be lessened.

---

[3] Still sometimes occurring in my first compositions in this style.

Justified already by historical development, the method of composing with twelve tones is also not without esthetic and theoretical support. On the contrary, it is just this support which advances it from a mere technical device to the rank and importance of a scientific theory.

Music is not merely another kind of amusement, but a musical poet's, a musical thinker's representation of musical ideas; these musical ideas must correspond to the laws of human logic; they are a part of what man can apperceive, reason and express. Proceeding from these assumptions, I arrived at the following conclusions:

THE TWO-OR-MORE-DIMENSIONAL SPACE IN WHICH MUSICAL IDEAS ARE PRESENTED IS A UNIT. Though the elements of these ideas appear separate and independent to the eye and the ear, they reveal their true meaning only through their cooperation, even as no single word alone can express a thought without relation to other words. All that happens at any point of this musical space has more than a local effect. It functions not only in its own plane, but also in all other directions and planes, and is not without influence even at remote points. For instance, the effect of progressive rhythmical subdivision, through what I call "the tendency of the shortest notes" to multiply themselves, can be observed in every classic composition.

A musical idea, accordingly, though consisting of melody, rhythm, and harmony, is neither the one nor the other alone, but all three together. The elements of a musical idea are partly incorporated in the horizontal plane as successive sounds, and partly in the vertical plane as simultaneous sounds. The mutual relation of tones regulates the succession of intervals as well as their association into harmonies; the rhythm regulates the succession of tones as well as the succession of harmonies and organizes phrasing. And this explains why, as will be shown later, a basic set of twelve tones (BS) can be used in either dimension, as a whole or in parts.

The basic set is used in diverse mirror forms. The composers of the last century had not employed such mirror forms as much as the masters of contrapuntal times; at least, they seldom did so consciously. Nevertheless, there exist examples, of which I want to mention only one from Beethoven's last String Quartet, Op. 135, in F major:

EXAMPLE 2

The original form, *a*, "Muss es sein," appears in *b* inverted and in major; *c* shows the retrograde form of this inversion, which, now reinverted in *d* and filled out with passing notes in *e*, results in the second phrase of the main theme.

Whether or not this device was used consciously by Beethoven does not matter at all. From my own experience I know that it can also be a subconsciously received gift from the Supreme Commander.

EXAMPLE 3

The two principal themes of my *Kammersymphonie* (Chamber Symphony) can be seen in Example 3 under *a* and *b*. After I had completed the work I worried very much about the apparent absence of any relationship between the two themes. Directed only by my sense of form and the stream of ideas, I had not asked such questions while composing; but, as usual with me, doubts arose as soon as I had finished. They went so far that I had already raised the sword for the kill, taken the red pencil of the censor to cross out the theme *b*. Fortunately, I stood by my inspiration and ignored these mental tortures. About twenty years later I saw the true relationship. It is of such a complicated nature that I doubt whether any composer would have cared deliberately to construct a theme in this way; but our subconscious does it involuntarily. In *c* the true principal tones of the theme are marked, and *d* shows that all the intervals ascend. Their correct inversion *e* produces the first phrase *f* of the theme *b*.

It should be mentioned that the last century considered such a procedure cerebral, and thus inconsistent with the dignity of genius. The very fact that there exist classical examples proves the foolishness of such an opinion. But the validity of this form of thinking is also demonstrated by the previously stated law of the unity of musical space, best formulated as follows: *the unity of musical space demands an absolute and unitary perception.* In this space, as in Swedenborg's heaven (described in Balzac's *Seraphita*) there is no absolute down, no right or left, forward or backward. Every musical configuration, every movement of tones has to be comprehended primarily as a mutual relation of sounds, of oscillatory vibrations, appearing at different places and times. To the imaginative and creative faculty, relations in the material sphere are as independent from directions or planes as material objects are, in their sphere, to our perceptive faculties. Just as our mind always recognizes, for instance, a knife, a bottle or a watch, regardless of its position, and can reproduce it in the imagination in every possible position, even so a musical creator's

mind can operate subconsciously with a row of tones, regardless of their direction, regardless of the way in which a
mirror might show the mutual relations, which remain a
given quantity.

VI

The introduction of my method of composing with twelve
tones does not facilitate composing; on the contrary, it makes
it more difficult. Modernistically-minded beginners often think
they should try it before having acquired the necessary technical equipment. This is a great mistake. The restrictions imposed on a composer by the obligation to use only one set
in a composition are so severe that they can only be overcome
by an imagination which has survived a tremendous number
of adventures. Nothing is given by this method; but much
is taken away.

It has been mentioned that for every new composition a
special set of twelve tones has to be invented. Sometimes a
set will not fit every condition an experienced composer can
foresee, especially in those ideal cases where the set appears
at once in the form, character, and phrasing of a theme. Recti-
fications in the order of tones may then become necessary.

In the first works in which I employed this method, I was
not yet convinced that the exclusive use of one set would
not result in monotony. Would it allow the creation of a sufficient number of characteristically differentiated themes,
phrases, motives, sentences, and other forms? At this time,
I used complicated devices to assure variety. But soon I discovered that my fear was unfounded; I could even base a
whole opera, *Moses and Aaron,* solely on one set; and I
found that, on the contrary, the more familiar I became with
this set the more easily I could draw themes from it. Thus,
the truth of my first prediction had received splendid proof.
One has to follow the basic set; but, nevertheless, one composes as freely as before.

VII

It has been mentioned that the basic set is used in mirror forms.

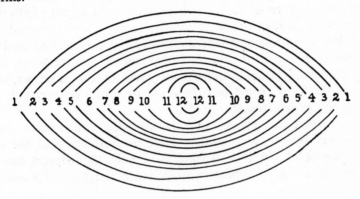

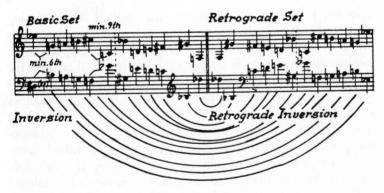

EXAMPLE 4

From the basic set, three additional sets are automatically derived: 1) the inversion; 2) the retrograde; and 3) the retrograde inversion.[4] The employment of these mirror forms corresponds to the principle of *the absolute and unitary per-*

---

4 BS means Basic Set; INV means inversion of the Basic Set; INV8, INV5, INV3, INV6 means inversion at the 8ve, 5th, minor 3rd, or major 6th from the beginning tone.

ception of musical space. The set of Example 4 is taken from the Wind Quintet, Op. 26, one of my first compositions in this style.

Later, especially in larger works, I changed my original idea, if necessary, to fit the following conditions: (see page 131) the inversion a fifth below of the first six tones, the antecedent, should not produce a repetition of one of these six tones, but should bring forth the hitherto unused six tones of the chromatic scale. Thus, the consequent of the basic set, the tones 7 to 12, comprises the tones of this inversion, but, of course, in a different order.

In Example 5 (page 118), the inversion a fifth below does not yet fulfill this condition. Here the antecedent of the BS plus that of the INV 5 consists of only 10 different tones, because c and b appear twice, while f and f# are missing.

VIII

In every composition preceding the method of composing with twelve tones, all the thematic and harmonic material is primarily derived from three sources: the tonality, the *basic motive* which in turn is a derivative of the tonality, and the *rhythm*, which is included in the basic motive. A composer's whole thinking was bound to remain in an intelligible manner around the central root. A composition which failed to obey these demands was considered "amateurish;" but a composition which adhered to it rigorously was never called "cerebral." On the contrary, the capacity to obey the principle instinctively was considered a natural condition of a talent.'

The time will come when the ability to draw thematic material from a basic set of twelve tones will be an unconditional prerequisite for obtaining admission into the composition class of a conservatory.

IX

The possibilities of evolving the formal elements of music— melodies, themes, phrases, motives, figures, and chords—out of a basic set are unlimited. In the following pages, a number of examples from my own works will be analyzed to reveal some of these possibilities. It will be observed that the succession of the tones according to their order in the set has always been strictly observed. One could perhaps tolerate a slight digression from this order (according to the same principle which allowed a remote variant in former styles)[6] in the later part of a work, when the set had already become familiar to the ear. However, one would not thus digress at the beginning of a piece.

The set is often divided into groups; for example, into two groups of six tones, or three groups of four, or four groups of three tones. This grouping serves primarily to provide a regularity in the distribution of the tones. The tones used in the melody are thereby separated from those to be used as accompaniment, as harmonies or as chords and voices demanded by the nature of the instrumentation, by the instrument, or by the character and other circumstances of a piece. The distribution may be varied or developed according to circumstances, in a manner comparable to the changes of what I call the "Motive of the Accompaniment."

X

The unlimited abundance of possibilities obstructs the systematic presentation of illustrations; therefore, an arbitrary procedure must be used here.

In the simplest case, a part of a theme, or even the entire theme, consists simply of a rhythmization and phrasing of a basic set and its derivatives, the mirror forms: inversion, retrograde, and retrograde inversion. While a piece usually begins with the basic set itself, the mirror forms and other derivatives, such as the eleven transpositions of all the four basic forms, are applied only later; the transpositions especially, like the modulations in former styles, serve to build subordinate ideas.

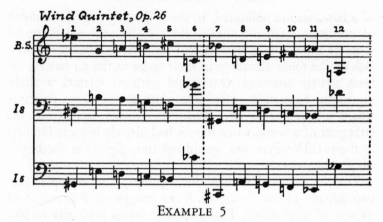

EXAMPLE 5

Example 5 shows the basic set (with its inversions in the octave and fifth) of my *Wind Quintet*, Op. 26.

Many themes of this work simply use the order of one of the basic forms.

EXAMPLE 6

The main theme of the first movement uses for its first phrase the first six tones, the antecedent; for its second phrase, the consequent of the BS. This example shows how an accompaniment can be built. As octave doubling should be avoided (see page 126), the accompanying of tones 1 - 6 with tones 7 - 12, and vice versa, is one way to fulfill this requirement.

EXAMPLE 7

Example 7 proves that the same succession of tones can produce different themes, different characters.

EXAMPLE 8

Example 8, the principal theme of the Rondo of this Quintet shows a new way of varying the repetitions of a theme. The production of such variants is not only necessary in larger forms, especially in Rondos, but useful also in smaller structures. While rhythm and phrasing significantly preserve the character of the theme so that it can easily be recognized, the tones and intervals are changed through a different use of BS and mirror forms. Mirror forms are used in the same way as the BS. But Example 9 shows a more complicated procedure.

Wind Quintet, Rondo, measures 117-124

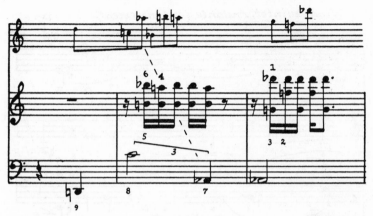

EXAMPLE 9

At first a transposition of the retrograde is used three times in succession to build melody and accompaniment of this subordinate theme of the Rondo from the same Quintet. The principal voice, the bassoon, uses three tones in each of the four phrases; the accompaniment uses only six tones, so that the phrases and the sets overlap each other, producing a sufficient degree of variety. There is a definite regularity in the distribution of the tones in this and the following Example 10, the Andante from the same Quintet.

EXAMPLE 10

Here also the form used, the BS, appears three times; here also, some of the tones appear in the principal voice (horn) while the others build a semi-contrapuntal melody in the bassoon.

Wind Quintet, Scherzo (2nd movement)

EXAMPLE 11

In the Scherzo of the same work (Example 11), the main theme starts with the fourth tone after the accompaniment has employed the preceding three tones of the BS. Here the accompaniment uses the same tones as the melody, but never at the same time.

EXAMPLE 12

In Example 12, inversion and retrograde inversion are combined into a contrapuntal unit which is worked out in the manner of the elaboration of the Rondo.

XI

Obviously, the requirement to use all the tones of the set is fulfilled whether they appear in the accompaniment or the melody. My first larger work in this style, the *Piano Suite*, Op. 25, already takes advantage of this possibility, as will be shown in some of the following examples. But the apprehension about the doubling of octaves caused me to take a special precaution.

EXAMPLE 13 and 13A

The BS as well as the inversion is transposed at the interval of a diminished fifth. This simple provision made it possible to use, in the Praeludium of this Suite, BS for the theme and the transposition for the accompaniment, without octave doubling.

EXAMPLE 14 and 14A

But in the Gavotte (Example 14) and the Intermezzo (Example 14a) this problem is solved by the first procedure mentioned above: the separate selection of the tones for their respective formal function, melody or accompaniment. In both cases a group of the tones appears too soon—9 - 12 in the left hand comes before 5 - 8. This deviation from the order is an irregularity which can be justified in two ways. The first of these has been mentioned previously: as the Gavotte is the second movement, the set has already become familiar. The second justification is provided by the subdivision of the BS into three groups of four tones. No change occurs within any one of these groups; otherwise, they are treated like independent small sets. This treatment is supported by the presence of a diminished fifth, D♭ - g, or g - D♭, as third and fourth tones in all forms of the set, and of another diminished fifth as seventh and eighth tones. This similarity, functioning as a relationship, makes the groups interchangeable.

EXAMPLE 15 and 15A

In the Menuet of the *Piano Suite* (Example 15) the melody begins with the fifth tone, while the accompaniment, much later, begins with the first tone.

The Trio of this Menuet (Example 15a) is a canon in which the difference between the long and short notes helps to avoid octaves.

The possibility of such canons and imitations, and even fugues and fugatos, has been overestimated by analysts of this style. Of course, for a beginner it might be as difficult to avoid octave doubling here as it is difficult for poor composers to avoid parallel octaves in the "tonal" style. But while a "tonal" composer still has to lead his parts into consonances or catalogued dissonances, a composer with twelve independent tones apparently possesses the kind of freedom which many would characterize by saying: "everything is allowed." "Everything" has always been allowed to two kinds of artists: to masters on the one hand, and to ignoramuses on the other. However, the meaning of composing in imitative style here is not the same as it is in counterpoint. It is only one of the ways of adding a coherent accompaniment, or subordinate voices, to the main theme, whose character it thus helps to express more intensively.

XII

The set of my *Variations for Orchestra,* Op. 31, is shown in Example 16a.

A work for orchestra must necessarily be composed of more voices than one for a smaller combination. Of course, many composers can manage with a small number of voices by doubling them in many instruments or in octaves, by breaking and doubling the harmony in many ways—sometimes thereby obscuring the presence of a content, sometimes making its absence clear. It must be admitted that most orchestral combinations do not promote what the artist calls unmixed, unbroken colors. The childish preference of the primitive ear for colors has kept a number of imperfect instruments in the orchestra, because of their individuality. More mature minds resist the temptation to become intoxicated by colors and prefer to be coldly convinced by the transparency of clear-cut ideas.

Avoidance of doubling in octaves automatically precludes the use of broken harmonies which contribute so much to the pleasant noise that is today called "sonority." Since I was educated primarily by playing and writing chamber music, my style of orchestration had long ago turned to thinness and transparency, in spite of contemporary influences. To provide for the worst seems better wisdom than to hope for the best. Therefore, I declined to take a chance, and, by making some slight changes, built the basic set so that its antecedent (see page 116), starting a minor third below, inverted itself into the remaining six tones of the full chromatic scale.

Variations, Op. 31

Variations, Op.31

EXAMPLE 16A and B

Besides, I used in many places a device, derived from double counterpoint of the tenth and twelfth, which allows the addition of parallel thirds to every part involved. By transposing BS a third up (BS3) and INV a third down (INV3), I obtained two more basic forms which allowed the addition of parallel thirds.

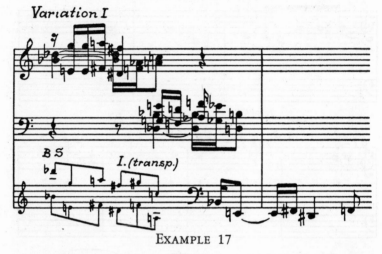

EXAMPLE 17

In the First Variation (Example 17) I used this device often, but not as often as I had expected. Very soon I recognized that my apprehension was unnecessary. Of the following examples, chosen at random to illustrate other peculiarities, none shows the addition of parallel thirds.

After an introduction successively revealing the tones of the BS and its INV3, the "Theme" of the Variations appears (Example 16). Built as a ternary form, it uses the tones of the BS and its three derivatives in strict order, without any omission or addition.

Variation V

EXAMPLE 18

The motive of the Fifth Variation is based on a transposition of the INV (INV8). Here are six independent parts built from only one set, comprising only the first two beats; the continuation carries on this system and finds ways to produce a satisfactory amount of variety.

EXAMPLE 19

The motive of the Sixth Variation is built from another transposition of the INV (INV6). It is composed of a contrapuntal combination of two melodic parts, using some tones of INV6 in the upper and others in the lower voice. This combination allows a great number of forms which furnish material for every demand of variation technique. New forms result through inversion of both voices (Example 20a) and other changes of their mutual positions such as, for instance, canonic imitation (Example 20b).

Variation VI

Variation VI

EXAMPLE 20 A and B

One should never forget that what one learns in school about history is the truth only insofar as it does not interfere with the political, philosophical, moral or other beliefs of those in whose interest the facts are told, colored or arranged. The same holds true with the history of music, and he who guilelessly believes all he is told—whether he be layman or professional—is defenseless and has to "take it," to take it as they give it. Of course, we know their guesses are no better than ours.

But unfortunately our historians are not satisfied with re-arranging the history of the past; they also want to fit the history of the present into their preconceived scheme. This forces them to describe the facts only as accurately as they see them, to judge them only as well as they understand them, to draw wrong conclusions from wrong premises, and to exhibit foggy visions of a future which exists only in their warped imaginations.

[137]

I am much less irritated than amused by the critical remark of one Dr. X, who says that I do not care for "sound."

"Sound," once a dignified quality of higher music, has deteriorated in significance since skillful workmen—orchestrators—have taken it in hand with the definite and undisguised intention of using it as a screen behind which the absence of ideas will not be noticeable. Formerly, sound had been the radiation of an intrinsic quality of ideas, powerful enough to penetrate the hull of the form. Nothing could radiate which was not light itself; and here only ideas are light.

Today, sound is seldom associated with idea. The superficially minded, not bothering with digesting the idea, notice especially the sound. "Brevity is essential to wit;" length, to most people, seems to be essential to sound. They observe it only if it lasts for a comparatively long time.

It is true that sound in my music changes with every turn of the idea—emotional, structural, or other. It is furthermore true that such changes occur in a more rapid succession than usual, and I admit that it is more difficult to perceive them simultaneously. The Seventh Variation offers just such obstacles to comprehension. But it is not true that the other kind of sonority is foreign to my music.

The rapid changes of the sonority in this Seventh Variation make it difficult for the listener to enjoy. The figure in the bassoon part continues for some time, while the instrumentation of the harmonies in eighth notes changes rapidly and continuously.

Variation VII

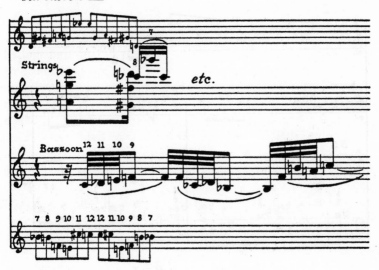

Finale

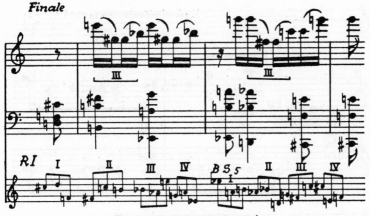

EXAMPLES 21, 22, 23, 24

Examples 21 - 24 show that a great multitude of thematic characters can be derived from one set. Various methods are, of course, applied. It may be worth while to mention that in Example 25,

Finale

EXAMPLE 25

as a homage to Bach, the notes B-flat, A, C, B, which spell, in German, BACH, were introduced as a contrapuntal addition to the principal thematic developments.

The main advantage of this method of composing with twelve tones is its unifying effect. In a very convincing way, I experienced the satisfaction of having been right about this when I once prepared the singers of my opera *Von Heute Auf Morgen* for a performance. The technique, rhythm and intonation of all these parts were tremendously difficult for them, though they all possessed absolute pitch. But suddenly one of the singers came and told me that since he had become familiar with the basic set, everything seemed easier for him. At short intervals all the other singers told me the same thing independently. I was very pleased with this, and, thinking it over, I found even greater encouragement in the following hypothesis:

Prior to Richard Wagner, operas consisted almost exclusively of independent pieces, whose mutual relation did not seem to be a musical one. Personally, I refuse to believe that in the great masterworks pieces are connected only by the superficial coherence of the dramatic proceedings. Even if these pieces were merely "fillers" taken from earlier works of the same composer, something must have satisfied the master's sense of form and logic. We may not be able to discover it, but certainly it exists. In music there is no form without logic, there is no logic without unity.

I believe that when Richard Wagner introduced his *Leitmotiv*—for the same purpose as that for which I introduced my Basic Set—he may have said: "Let there be unity."

A Dangerous Game [1]

THERE ARE a great many categories of collaborators in Germany and in the conquered countries. One must distinguish between the many who have been forced to collaborate and those who have done so voluntarily. There are others, besides, who simply "missed the bus," who would have preferred to emigrate rather than bow to dictates, if it had not become too late for them to do so. And there are also those whose stupid egotism led them to believe that evil could happen only to others while they themselves would be spared. Some did only what they were ordered to do, others functioned as agitators, prosecuting those who did not conform to the prescribed style, and based their conduct on the theoretical party line.

With the thought in mind that the captain in *Carmen* is not intended to represent a coward but simply a man who yields to the argument of the guns which confront him, it may be said that only those should be authorized to blame the forced collaborator who have themselves proved fearless before the menace of the concentration camp and of torture. People like that of course also exist.

Curiously, few realize that politics, a nice topic to talk about, is a rather dangerous game into which one should enter only if he is aware that his life and that of his opponent are at stake and if he is willing to pay for his conviction— even that price.

Artists generally deal with this problem as thoughtlessly as if it were merely a controversy on artistic matters; just as if they were discussing merely "art for art's sake" as contrasted with "objectivity in art." Even in such arguments a partici-

1 Published as part of a symposium "On Artists and Collaboration" in *Modern Music*, XXII, 2, November-December, 1944.

pant's life may be at stake. I wonder whether Richard Wagner knew that he would be living in exile as an outlaw for so many years when, because of artistic corruption, he participated in setting the Dresden Hoftheater on fire.

On the other hand, very few of those who emigrated can ask to be honored for their political or artistic straightforwardness. Most of them had no other chance of being spared, either because of their race or that of their matrimonial partner. Many had been politically implicated and others came under the ban of "Kultur-Bolschewismus." There are probably not many who emigrated voluntarily; and even among such "real" emigrés there are some who tried hard to come to an agreement with the powers only to give up in the end.

Yet despite the fact that little personal merit attaches to the inability of many to swim with the official current (*Gleichschaltung*), there is this to be said for them: they all had to abandon their homes, their positions, their countries, their friends, their business, their fortune. They all had to go abroad, to try to start life anew, and generally at a much lower level of living, of influence, of esteem; many even had to change their occupations and to suffer humiliation.

There may be no merit in all that; still, if those who had to do it could do it—why should not others also have preferred to preserve their honesty, their integrity, their character, by taking upon themselves of their own free will the suffering of an emigré, like those who had no other way?

That would have been of some merit!

I am inclined to say:

Those who here acted like politicians are politicians and should be treated in the same manner in which politicians are treated.

Those who did not so act should escape punishment.

But considering the low mental and moral standards of artists in general, I would say:

Treat them like immature children.

Call them fools and let them escape.

Eartraining through Composing [1]

I

SUPPOSE someone paid a visit to the ancient buildings of Rome or the famous pictures in the Louvre in Paris, or read a poem by Goethe or an involved mystery story by Poe. What would his reactions be?

In Rome he might dream of the mighty Roman empire, of the slaves who built its monuments, the citizens who attended the public games. At the Louvre he might again surrender to his imagination. A religious painting would remind him of Biblical stories, mythological sculpture would turn his thoughts to paganism. Reading the poem by Goethe, he would associate it with the life of this great man. Remembering the *Sorrows of Werther*, he would go on to think of the opera, *Werther*, by Massenet—who also wrote *Manon*, which he likes better.

A nice dream!

And he would be quite right not to resist the temptation of his imagination. But would the same attitude be advisable while he was reading a mystery story? Dreaming of more or less related subjects, interesting or beautiful though they be, could he absorb and remember the details which simultaneously hide and reveal the murderer?

It is not too serious *not* to discover the solution of such crimes. But if the first examples did not show the point I am about to make, then the case of the detective story must have made it clear: one cannot do justice to a work of art while allowing one's imagination to wander to other subjects, re-

---

[1] *Modern Music*, XXIII, 3, Fall 1946.

lated or not. In the face of works of art one must not dream, but one must try hard to grasp their meaning.

II

"Music Appreciation" often gives a music student not much more than the perfume of a work, that narcotic emanation of music which affects the senses without involving the mind. No one listening to popular music would be satisfied with such an impression. There is no doubt about the moment when a man starts to like a song or dance. It is when he begins to sing or whistle it—in other words when he is able to remember it. If this criterion is applied to serious music, it becomes clear that one does not like more than its perfume unless one can keep it in mind.

Remembering is the first step toward understanding. To understand as simple a sentence as "The table is round" requires keeping the *table* in mind. Forget the table and only the perfume of the sentence remains. Historical facts, biographies of authors and performers, anecdotes of their lives, pathetic, humorous, interesting or instructive, may be of some value to people who are otherwise deaf to the effects of music. But all this cannot help anyone to absorb and remember the content.

Of course the best way to train a musical ear is to expose it to as much serious music as possible. Musical culture would spread faster if people would read music, play music or even listen to music much more than they do today. Extensive familiarity with serious music is the foremost requirement of musical culture. But even this is not enough without thorough ear-training.

Ear-training, in the narrow sense, is practiced in high schools and colleges with excellent results. Good methods have been developed, but, like teaching techniques in other musical subjects, they have become too abstract, to some extent have lost contact with the original purpose. A trained ear is valuable, but not especially so if the ear is the gateway to the auditory sense rather than the musical mind. Like harmony, counterpoint and other theoretical studies, ear-training is not an end in itself, but only a step towards musicianship.

One often hears the question, "Why teach composition to people who will never try it again after their student days are over, people who have neither creative ability nor the creative impulse, for whom it is a nightmare to have to express something in an idiom quite foreign to their minds?"

The answer is this: just as almost anyone can be trained to draw, paint, write an essay or deliver a lecture, it must also be possible to make people with even less than mediocre gifts use the means of musical composition in a sensitive manner. The prospect of having to listen to their musical products makes such a possibility seem rather dubiously desirable, and it is certainly not the purpose of theory teaching to produce a surplus of unwanted composers. Still, every good musician should submit to such training. How can one enjoy a game without understanding its fine points, without knowing when the ball is sliced or curved, without an idea of strategy or tactics? And yet there are performers who simply do not know the bare construction, not to mention the subtleties of musical pieces!

Understanding the fine points—that is, understanding the game at all—demands a thorough preparation. Harmony, counterpoint and form need not be taught as branches of esthetics or history. A few illustrations will show how this training can be used to better purpose.

If a student of harmony not only writes his examples, but also plays them afterwards, his ear will become acquainted with a number of facts. He will realize that chords are used in root positions and inversions and that there is a difference in structural weight between them. And when he hears a classical fermata on a six-four chord, he will not applaud, knowing that this cannot be the end of the piece. Even someone with absolute pitch might mistake the ending of the first section of a symphony for the end of the movement if he knew nothing of the structural functions of tonality. Sometimes a deceptive cadence is similarly misunderstood.

Knowledge of harmony alone will not suffice to correct such errors. Further studies are necessary to fortify that knowledge and to anchor it firmly in instinct. Even people without absolute pitch can learn to recognize modulatory sections. Why should a composer write such sections at all if they have no effect upon the layman? A well-trained student of harmony will also have at least some acquaintance with the effects of centrifugal harmonies.

The study of counterpoint develops the capacity for listening to more than one voice. A listener who hears in a fugue only the repetitions of the theme may well complain of monotony. But if he also perceives the accompanying voices, which are often second and third subjects, he will come closer to understanding the true nature of contrapuntal composition. Even in homophonic compositions there are cases where one must hear more than the principal voice. Many extensions in the music of Mozart and Brahms are produced by a movement of the harmony contradictory to the melody, an effect which is lost on anyone who listens to the melody alone. Every note a master has written should be perceived. How much pleasure it gives the connoisseur to watch the second violin in a Mozart quartet, as it accommodates itself to the first, assists or contradicts, expresses sympathy or antipathy by characteristic interjections!

III

These examples may already have given a clue to how much more might be achieved through the study of form and orchestration.

It is a great mistake to believe that the object of form is beauty. There is no beauty in eight measures because they are eight, no lack of beauty in ten. Mozart's asymmetry is not less beautiful than Beethoven's symmetry. The principal function of form is to advance our understanding. Music should be enjoyed. Undeniably, understanding offers man one of the most enjoyable pleasures. And though the object of form is not beauty, by providing comprehensibility, form produces beauty. An apple tree does not exist in order to give us apples, but it produces them nevertheless.

Forms are primarily organizations to express ideas in a comprehensible manner. An attempt at self-expression is a useful approach to understanding the methods of the great composers. A student knows by experience that the repetition of a section may on one occasion be good, useful or inevitable, on another poor, unnecessary or monotonous, and he will recognize the meaning of repetition in the works of others. Repetition, if not monotonous, helps to convey a musical idea. Anyone trained to vary the basic motive of his own composition will probably be able to follow a complicated melody without involuntarily dreaming of irrelevant images.

It is the organization of a piece which helps the listener to keep the idea in mind, to follow its development, its growth, its elaboration, its fate. If you have been taught to provide your themes with limits, to distinguish principal and subordinate ideas, to combine fluency with lucidity, to divide distinctly into parts what cannot be conceived undivided, you will know how to make use of these earmarks in masterpieces as symbols to remember. The theme of the fourth movement of Beethoven's Quartet in A Minor, Op. 132, consists amazingly of ten measures and, more amazingly still, in its tenth measure reaches a provisional ending on the seventh degree of A minor: G major. Scarcely a musician would recognize the singularity of such a procedure if he had not been taught that themes like this ought to consist of eight measures only, and to end on the first, third or fifth degree. But anyone who knows this will easily recognize the theme whenever it appears in the development.

Without remembering, how could we understand variations? When a composer calls his piece *Variations on X,* he obviously wants us to understand every variation as a derivative of his chosen theme. The Haydn theme of Brahms' *Variations* has an "A" section which consists of a ten-measure period characteristically subdivided at the first measure. It is difficult not to recognize this in the variations. Furthermore, the third section is unusual in that it is prolonged by means of an extension. No one, at first hearing, can grasp all the fine points of Brahms' variation technique, the harmonic and contrapuntal combinations, the many ways in which he treats the unevenness of his five-measure sections. Perhaps all this is not absolutely necessary for an adequate response to the music. But it is certainly a good approach to what the composer himself wants to tell us.

Composing trains the ear to recognize what should be kept in mind, and thus helps the understanding of musical ideas. Characteristic deviations from the norm, irregularities, will be guides in the no-man's-land of great ideas.

Now to speak of orchestration. My concept of color is not the usual one. Color, like light and shadow in the physical world, expresses and limits the forms and sizes of objects. Sometimes these elements serve as a camouflage. A musician likewise might wish to hide something. For instance, like a good tailor, he might wish to hide the seams where sections are sewn together. In general, however, lucidity is the first purpose of color in music, the aim of the orchestration of every true artist. I do not wish to be a killjoy, but I must confess that I find the delight in colors somewhat overrated. Perhaps the art of orchestration has become too popular, and interesting-sounding pieces are often produced for no better reason than that which dictates the making of typewriters and fountain pens in different colors.

IV

It is obvious that not even a small percentage of music students will become composers. They cannot and they should not. It is also evident that many would-be composers and mu-

sicians who, through some study, have acquired a superficial
knowledge of music, may presume to judge the activities of
good artists and real creators. This is where a correct attitude
on the part of the teacher becomes most important. He must
convince his students that the study of composition will not
make them experts or acknowledged judges, that its only purpose is to help them understand music better, to obtain that
pleasure which is inherent in the art. The possession of an ear
trained through composing should not entitle a man to humili-
ate his innocent and less fortunate neighbor. It should give
him only one pleasure: the pleasure of balance between the
joy he expects from music and the joy he actually receives.

Heart and Brain in Music [1]

BALZAC in his philosophical story "Seraphita" describes one of his characters as follows: "Wilfred was a man thirty years of age. Though strongly built, his proportions did not lack harmony. He was of medium height as is the case with almost all men who tower above the rest. His chest and his shoulders were broad and his neck was short, like that of men whose heart must be within the domain of the head."

No doubt all those who supposedly create cerebrally—philosophers, scientists, mathematicians, constructers, inventors, theorists, architects—keep their emotions under control and preserve the coolness of their heads even though imagination will often inspire them. But it is not generally agreed that poets, artists, musicians, actors, and singers should admit the influence of a brain upon their emotions.

Only a few decades ago it was the standard opinion that a poet, and especially a lyric poet, was distinguished not only by long hair and a dirty collar but also by his habit of assuming an interesting pose. In place of a sober and direct word, he was expected to use one which only circumscribed an idea or a fact and, if possible, obscured both a little, befogged their meaning and appearance. Thus they appeared as something out of a dream, suggesting that the reader—no, not that he fall asleep, but only that he dream without sleeping.

Though such viewpoints no longer prevail, similar outmoded misconceptions are still in circulation. One such misconception is the general belief that the constituent qualities of music belong to two categories as regards their origin: to the heart or to the brain, with the exception of some products in which both might have a word to say.

[1] *The Works of the Mind* (The University of Chicago Press, 1947).

Those qualities in which a listener likes to recognize his own heart are those which he deems to have originated in the emotions of a composer: the beautiful melody or phrase, the beautiful—or, at least, sweet—sound, the beautiful harmony.

Those qualities of a less heart-warming nature, such as dynamic contrasts, changes of tempo, accentuation, features of rhythm and accompaniment, and, most of all, the finesses of organization—these seem to be ascribed to the cooperation of heart and brain and might be classified rather as "interesting," arousing the interest of a listener without considerable appeal to his feelings.

The third group arouses neither so much feeling nor interest, but, if it should accelerate the heart-beat, it is because of the admiration, the awe, in which it is held. Counterpoint, contrapuntal style, is definitely attributed to the brain. It is honored by the highest appreciation but tolerated only if it does not destroy the warmth of the dreams into which the charm of the beautiful has led the listener.

I believe that a real composer writes music for no other reason than that it pleases him. Those who compose because they want to please others, and have audiences in mind, are not real artists. They are not the kind of men who are driven to say something whether or not there exists one person who likes it, even if they themselves dislike it. They are not creators who must open the valves in order to relieve the interior pressure of a creation ready to be born. They are merely more or less skillful entertainers who would renounce composing if they could not find listeners.

Real music by a real composer might produce every kind of impression without aiming to. Simple and beautiful melodies, salty rhythms, interesting harmony, sophisticated form, complicated counterpoint—the real composer writes them with the ease with which one writes a letter. "As if he were writing a letter"—this is what my comrades in the Austrian army said admiringly when, in the barracks, I wrote some music for a party given by the company. That this was not a remarkably beautiful piece but only one of average craftmanship does not make any difference, because it often takes as much time to compose a letter as to write music. I personally belong to those who generally write very fast, whether it is "cerebral" counterpoint or "spontaneous" melody.

Most of the friends of my youth were also fast writers. For instance, Alexander von Zemlinsky, composer of many successful operas, while still studying composition at the Vienna Conservatory, prepared at the same time for a competition in piano which he later won. He had a peculiar method of using his time rationally, since he was forced to give many piano lessons in order to earn a living. He would alternately compose and practice the piano. Writing in ink one page of music, he had to wait for the page to dry. This interval of time only could he spare for practice. A busy life!

A week was generally considered just sufficient time to start and finish a sonata movement. But I once wrote all four movements of a string quartet within this length of time. A song for voice and piano might have required one to three hours—three hours, if you were unfortunately caught with a long poem.

I composed three-fourths of both the second and the fourth movements of my String Quartet No. 2 in one-and-a-half days each. I completed the half-hour music of my opera *Erwartung* in fourteen days. Several times I wrote two or three pieces of *Pierrot Lunaire* and the song-cycle *Hängende Gärten* in a day. I could mention many more such examples.

Thus it will be as astonishing to you as it was to all my friends when I came with the score of *Verklärte Nacht* and showed them one particular measure on which I had worked a full hour, though I had written the entire score of four hundred and fifteen measures in three weeks. This measure is indeed a little complicated since, according to the artistic conviction of this period (the post-Wagnerian), I wanted to express the idea *behind* the poem, and the most adequate means to that end seemed a complicated contrapuntal combination: a leitmotiv and its inversion played simultaneously (Example 1).

EXAMPLE 1: *Verklärte Nacht*

This combination was not the product of a spontaneous inspiration but of an extra-musical intention, of a cerebral reflection. The technical labor which required so much time was in adding such subordinate voices as would soften the harsh frictions of this combination.

Of course there is always the possibility that in the midst of a composition there might suddenly emerge new reasons for persuading a composer to engage in such a venture. One of the most frequent of such reasons is artistic ambition, the artist's sense of honor. Indeed, the aim of an artist to elaborate profoundly upon his ideas, especially if it makes the task more difficult for him and even if it makes it more difficult for his listeners—this aim should not be condemned even if the cerebral procedure causes loss of the surface beauty. Besides, an artist need not necessarily fail if he has started something to which inspiration has not forced him. Often enough inspiration intervenes spontaneously and gives its blessing un-demanded.

It often happens to a composer that he writes down a melody in one uninterrupted draft and with a perfection that requires no change and offers no possibility of improvement. It has occurred often enough to me. For instance, in this melody from my String Quartet No. 2, I certainly did not make the slightest change (Example 2).

EXAMPLE 2: String Quartet No. 2

I was certainly no less directed by inspiration when I started my First Chamber Symphony (*Kammersymphonie*). I had a perfect vision of the whole work—of course, not in all its details but in its main features. But, while I wrote many of the subordinate themes later in *one* draft, I had to work very hard to shape the beginning. I have copied here some of the phases and metamorphoses through which the first two main ideas had to pass before I was satisfied (Example 3).

EXAMPLE 3 A, B, C, D: *Kammersymphonie,*

Principal Theme 3

A —Shows the one rhythmic and melodic configuration, which reappears in all sketches.

Aa—Shows an attempt at a continuation, which is quite unbalanced but contains one rhythm (Aa) which does not disappear any more.

B —Already brings the ascending whole tones, though in a broader rhythmization, and the triplets (*) which also appear in the following sketch 2C and in the final form.

EXAMPLE 3 E, F, G, H, I, J: *Kammersymphonie,*

E, F, G, H, I, J

Principal Theme 5

E —This first sketch already contains four features which are used in all following sketches and also in the final form (3-J). The melodic form marked *a* consists here only of four notes. But already the next sketch adds the fifth tone (A*b*). There is also under *b* the syncopated rhythm (⋏), under *c* the characteristic leap of a ninth, c to d, and the harmonic progression based on fourth chords, marked (*).

G to I—Preserve the first 4½ measures and try to continue in various ways. The final form is then given in Example 3-J.

In all these cases there was no problem which one would call complicated. There was no combination of voices whose contrapuntal relation required adaptation, as in the example from *Verklärte Nacht*. In these first notations, there were even no harmonic progressions which demanded control. There was at hand from the start a sufficient amount of motival forms and their derivatives, rather too much than too little. The task, therefore, was to retard the progress of development in order to enable the average good listener to keep in mind what preceded so as to understand the consequences. To keep within bounds and to balance a theme whose character, tempo, expression, harmonic progression, and motival contents displayed a centrifugal tendency: this was here the task. If one compares the difficult labor required in this case with the great ease with which most of the other themes were conceived, one might conclude that inspiration at times makes a gift to a composer in a perfect form, which at other times is denied him. In both cases it was not complexity which stood in the way of perfection, nor was it the heart which erred nor the brain which corrected.

In order to give an idea how such themes look when conceived spontaneously and written without correction, I refer the reader to the subordinate theme of the *Kammersymphonie* (No. 21, pp. 22-23 in the score). Or Example 4, from the same work, will also illustrate this point.

EXAMPLE 4: *Kammersymphonie*, Adagio Theme

There are other cases which might even increase the confusion and make the determination of the share of heart or brain, of inspiration or labor, more difficult.

Some forty years ago I was composing my String Quartet No. 1, Op. 7. Usually taking morning walks, I composed in my mind forty to eighty measures complete in almost every detail. I needed only two or three hours to copy down these large sections from memory. From such a section of about eighty measures (which even a fast writer could not copy in less time than it took me to compose them) I want to give some illustrations and explain some of the intricate complexities involved.

The first violin plays a passage in measures 100-103 (p. 46 in the score):

This is repeated in 107-10 (p. 46):

79

And again in 40-43 (p. 48):

These three statements differ in their accompaniment and harmonization and lead to different endings: the first to D minor, the second to D major, the third to D major chords.

The pizzicato in 103-4 (p. 46) is part of the Scherzo theme, and is used in many transformations. In measures 1-11, after H (pp. 46-47), it accompanies a transformation of the main theme:

and in 43-46 (p. 48) a variant of it is used similarly:

Note also the independent voice leading in 19-26 (p. 47):

And a similar example will be found in 63-70 (pp. 49-50). Besides the examples given here, there are numerous other contrapuntal combinations; and doubtless the entire section is of a texture which one must call complicated.

One who assumes that counterpoint is cerebral while melody is spontaneous would be forced, in the face of these two examples, to conclude that cerebral products can be written faster than those of spontaneous feeling. But nothing could be more erroneous; the one as well as the other may require much or little work. Whether much or little labor is necessary depends on circumstances over which we have no control. Only one thing is certain, at least to me: without inspiration *neither* could be accomplished.

There are times when I am unable to write a single example of simple counterpoint in two voices, such as I ask sophomores to do in my classes. And, in order to write a *good* example of this sort, I must receive the cooperation of inspiration. I am in this respect much weaker than some of my pupils who write good or poor counterpoint without any kind of inspiration.

However, having been educated in the sphere of Brahmsian influence (I was only a little over twenty-two when Brahms died), like many others I followed his example. "When I do not feel like composing, I write some counterpoint." Unfortunately, Brahms destroyed everything he did not consider worthy of publication before he died. This is regrettable, for to be allowed to look into the workshop of such a conscientious man would be extremely instructive. One would see how often he had worked hard to prepare his basic ideas for those conclusions he foresaw. "A good theme is a gift of God," he said; and he concluded with a word of Goethe: "Deserve it in order to possess it."

One thing seems certain: Brahms' mental gymnastics were certainly not of an easygoing sort. We know that it was his habit on his Sunday excursions in the Wienerwald to prepare "enigmatic canons" whose solutions occupied his companions for several hours. Subsequently I was stimulated to try also the difficult types of canons. There were some which required much work, as, for instance, the following example. Perhaps this mirror canon required such a painful effort because my heart refused to cooperate (Example 5).

EXAMPLE 5: Mirror Canon

Even though the purpose of such things is not music but only gymnastics, I must have been inspired, or at least in a good mood, when I wrote the Mirror Canon for String Quartet in about an hour (Example 6).

EXAMPLE 6: Mirror Canon for String Quartet

But what assisted me in writing these canons could never have been inspiration of the same kind which produced melodies like that of the Adagio section of my String Quartet No. 1, Op. 7 (Example 7).

EXAMPLE 7: Adagio Theme, Op. 7

It is perhaps necessary to show also some melodies of my later period, especially of the composition with twelve tones, which has earned me the title of constructionist, engineer, mathematician, etc., meaning that these compositions are produced exclusively by the brain without the slightest participation of something like a human heart. As an example from my later period, I quote here the beginning of my Piano Concerto, Op. 42 (Example 8').

EXAMPLE 8: Concerto for Piano and Orchestra, Op. 42

(Reproduction of Orchestra for a Second Piano by Edward Steuermann)

An unprejudiced musician will easily find many more such melodies in my latest work. See, for instance, the Intermezzo from my String Quartet No. 3, Op. 30, and the Andante Grazioso of the Violin Concerto, Op. 36.

EXAMPLE 9: Third String Quartet, Intermezzo

EXAMPLE 10: Andante, Violin Concerto

Assuming that a composer is at least entitled to like his themes (even though it may not be his duty to publish only what he himself likes), I dare say that I have shown here only melodies, themes, and sections from my works which I deemed to be good if not beautiful. Some of them were produced with ease; others are complicated. But one cannot pretend that the complicated ones required hard work or that the simple ones were always easily produced. Also, one cannot pretend that it makes any difference whether the examples derive from a spontaneous emotion or from a cerebral effort.

Unfortunately, there is no record that classic masters made much ado about the greater or lesser efforts needed for different tasks. Perhaps they wrote everything with the same ease, or, as one might suspect in the case of Beethoven, with the same great effort, as Beethoven's sketch books prove.

But one thing seems to be clear: whether its final aspect is that of simplicity or of complexity, whether it was composed swiftly and easily or required hard work and much time, the

[178]

finished work gives no indication of whether the emotional or the cerebral constituents have been determinant.

It is necessary to remember that frequently the elaboration of unaccompanied themes and melodies in the examples I have shown required from three to seven sketches, while some of the contrapuntal sections were composed in a very short time.

It seems to me that I anticipated the solution to this problem in the very beginning of this essay with the quotation from Balzac: "The heart must be within the domain of the head."

It is not the heart alone which creates all that is beautiful, emotional, pathetic, affectionate, and charming; nor is it the brain alone which is able to produce the well-constructed, the soundly organized, the logical, and the complicated. First, everything of supreme value in art must show heart as well as brain. Second, the real creative genius has no difficulty in controlling his feelings mentally; nor must the brain produce only the dry and unappealing while concentrating on correctness and logic.

But one might become suspicious of the sincerity of works which incessantly exhibit their heart; which demand our pity; which invite us to dream with them of a vague and undefined beauty and of unfounded, baseless emotions; which exaggerate because of the absence of reliable yardsticks; whose simplicity is want, meagerness, and dryness; whose sweetness is artificial and whose appeal attains only to the surface of the superficial. Such works only demonstrate the complete absence of a brain and show that this sentimentality has its origin in a very poor heart.

Criteria for the Evaluation of Music

IN THE BEST SELLERS of 150 or 200 years ago there frequently appeared a character—an old cavalier, generally no less than a marquis, whose extreme generosity perplexed and astounded both his fellow characters and the reading public of that day. Whether or not such a character ever really existed, the grandeur of his generosity was impressive. When he met with a slight accident—whether to himself, to his horse, or only to his equipage—he would reward the person who came to his rescue by throwing to him his whole purse, which, of course, contained nothing but gold pieces—small change his hands would not touch. On other occasions he might disperse a few handfuls of louis d'or among a crowd. Such was his generosity in minor accidents.

Imagine then what he might have done in case of a serious accident! He then might have taken the rescuer to his castle and either made him heir to his fortune and title, or offered him his sister in marriage. Even if she were not the most beautiful woman in the world, she was full of charm, and, besides, would have a respectable dowry!

At any rate, as a true nobleman he insisted on paying a price which surpassed the value of the service rendered, and he would have been ashamed to disappoint the faith of lower-class people in the generosity of the nobility. On the other hand, one must not forget that, fictitious or real, this nobleman was convinced of the inexhaustibility of his fortune, was convinced that he need not care what price he paid, and was only afraid to pay less than his social rank required.

What a man! What people! What times!

While the nobleman not only did not ask the price of what he bought, but, rather, did not want to know it, we poor people are bound to know prices in advance. All the same, whether we buy a house, a pair of shoes, or an automobile—we must know their value and whether it justifies the price. We must know whether the house has the desired number of rooms, whether the neighborhood is good, how high the taxes are, whether there is a chance of selling it without too great a loss after some years, and so forth. Similar questions will be asked about the shoes. They must fit, they should not be of an obsolete fashion, the material should be adequate, etc. We would also refuse to pay more for an automobile than it is worth, even if we possessed the money, because, of course, our revenues are not inexhaustible. Moreover, we hate to pay more for a thing than it is worth—if possible, we prefer to pay less. This is—on the average—human nature, and people of all ranks behave similarly. They love to pay less than it is worth.

If we justify such caution in the case of a house, a pair of shoes, and an automobile, merits or shortcomings of which are no secret and do not require the judgment of an expert, how much more is caution justified in the case of art objects, where criteria of evaluation are really only within the domain of the experts and where experts are as rare as a good judgment.

True, the styles of houses, of shoes and of automobiles change, but at least, as they serve a definite purpose, their useability remains the same, and one who judges only that will not fail.

But style in art changes approximately every ten to fifteen years. And almost inevitably evaluation changes with style. One of the safest methods of acquiring attention is to do something which differs from the usual, and few artists have the stamina to escape this temptation. I must confess that I belonged to those who did not care much about originality. I used to say: "I always attempted to produce something quite conventional, but I failed, and it always, against my will, became something unusual!" How right, then, is a music lover who refuses to appreciate music which even the composer did not want to write!

And is it unreasonable that one who commissions his portrait hates to look as an expressionist painter, whose idea is based on psychoanalysis, thinks it should look? Others, again, do not want to appear as victims of a candid camera's sincerity. It may be the morals, the philosophy, the political viewpoint of a writer to which you are opposed. It may be old-fashioned for an author to come personally to the foreground as Goethe did in *Die Wanderjahre,* when at a certain point he inserts a story without any coherence with the preceding, saying ". . . because we want to prove that we are not lacking in inventiveness"—the inventiveness to produce a nice little story. Strindberg would not have done this; perhaps Balzac would have, or perhaps Shaw—in one of his prefaces but not in the text.

One may wonder, if the great Goethe did it, can it be entirely wrong? And should such a procedure be entirely excluded from art? And, if so, only because it is oldfashioned? Or perhaps because "to show inventiveness" is no proper reason for inclusion in a work of art, because there should appear only that which derives from and is related to the subject, at least indirectly?

But what if the continuation were to disclose the relation of this story with the subject?

There might still remain the objection to the manner in which it is introduced—"in order to show inventiveness"—which is one of the personal interests of an author, but should manifest itself silently. Then the reader, with enthusiastic admiration, might exclaim: "What richness of imagination and inventiveness."

It seems that the man in the street and other uninitiated people have still some access to the evaluation offered by the subject, or the object, or the story of works of literature, painting, sculpture, architecture and other arts. How inadequate such viewpoints are can best be seen in the case of the great number of painters who have already been admitted into the Academy of Immortals: the El Grecos, the Van Goghs, the Gauguins, the Kandinskys, the Kokoschkas, the Matisses, the Picassos.

Since changes of style in the arts do not always mean development, it might be extremely difficult to establish criteria which remain valid in every period of art. But the futility of evaluation deriving from external criteria remains evident throughout the centuries.

At least a wrong evaluation can be based on superficial judgment in the aforementioned arts. No such thing is possible in music. There is no story, no subject, no object, no moral, no philosophy or politics which one might like or hate. Rejection of musical works in the last one and a half centuries has been based primarily on features which obstructed comprehensibility: too rich modulation, use of dissonances, complicated formulation of ideas. It was the time when towns were growing into cities, when the development of industrialism was bringing fresh but uninitiated people into the cities. It was the time when concert halls had to become larger and larger, because more people became participants in the audiences.

Before this time audiences had been small and had consisted solely of music lovers most of whom were able to play what they liked, many of whom had at least semi-professional knowledge, if not more. Their judgment was then to some degree based on terms which today only the experts are entitled to use—though also others do. Musicianship of such high degree enables recognition of evaluating criteria. Knowing music meant knowing it—at least partly—from memory. Many persons were able to remember a piece after a single hearing. Do not forget that Mozart wrote down the forbidden music of Allegri's *Miserere* after hearing it only once.

Yes, the role of memory in music evaluation is more important than most people realize. It is perhaps true that one starts to understand a piece only when one can remember it at least partially. But memory must be nursed and given an opportunity to function. Before the first World War I met a man who told me that he had seen *The Merry Widow* twenty times. And during the war, when I conducted Beethoven's Ninth Symphony, a man came into the artists' room to tell me that this was the fiftieth performance of the work he had heard from beginning to end. Imagine how well these people knew every note of their favorite music!

One could not, of course, expect such capacities of freshly acquired devotees of the arts. While J. S. Bach was allowed to write music of a kind which in its real values only the expert is capable of understanding, very soon the composers in the eighteenth and nineteenth centuries came to feel that their real independence had gone. Even a Beethoven, democratic as he was, must have felt it. But Mozart was told, after the first performance of his *Don Giovanni* in Vienna, by the Emperor Joseph II: "This is no music for our Viennese." "No music for our Viennese?" At that time already it was not the highest quality of art Mozart should produce, but he was supposed to express himself as broadly as popular understanding required.

I would not contend that later composers consciously gave in to these popular demands for comprehensibility—demands which do not correspond entirely to the demands of higher art. But there is no doubt that much in Schubert's melodic construction—his juxtaposition of motives, which are only melodically varied, but rhythmically very similar—accommodated, probably instinctively, to the popular feeling. As a true child of his time, he reflected involuntarily the feeling of his contemporaries. Robert Schumann's style is a further proof of the same kind of accommodation; his extremely frequent repetitions of a rhythmic character indicate this.

EXAMPLE 1: Melodies of Schubert and Schumann

   a. Schubert, Scherzo, Piano Sonata in D Major
   b. Schumann, *Arabesque*

Accommodations to the popular demands became even more imperative when Wagner's evolution of harmony expanded into a revolution of form. While preceding composers and even his contemporary, Johannes Brahms, repeated phrases, motives and other structural ingredients of themes only in varied forms, if possible in the form of what I call *developing variation*, Wagner, in order to make his themes suitable for memorability, had to use sequences and semi-sequences, that is, unvaried or slightly varied repetitions differing in nothing essential from first appearances, except that they are exactly transposed to other degrees.

EXAMPLE 2: Wagner Sequences

Why there is a lesser merit in such procedure than in variation is obvious, because variation requires a new and special effort. But the damage of this inferior method of construction to the art of composing was considerable. With very few exceptions, all followers and even opponents of Wagner became addicts of this more primitive technique: Bruckner, Hugo Wolf, Richard Strauss, and even Debussy and Puccini.

A new technique had to be created, and in this development Max Reger, Gustav Mahler, and also I myself played a role. But the destructive consequences did not cease because of that. And unfortunately many of today's composers, instead of connecting ideas through developing variation, thus showing consequences derived from the basic idea and remaining within the boundaries of human thinking and its demands of logic, produce compositions which become longer and broader only by numerous unvaried repetitions of a few phrases.

I have made here the grave mistake of calling a criterion of compositorial technique "destructive" as if it were now proven for all time to come that such a procedure is worthless.

How can a house differ from every other house and express a definite architectural idea, if there is as little variety in its material—bricks—as there is in the unvaried repetitions of a phrase? Need it be disadvantageous to use motives, phrases, and other units in a manner as uninfluential on the final form as bricks on a building?

Could not the case of Beethoven's *Pastorale Symphony* be considered as one where harmonies are comparable to bricks, because harmonies of only one kind are used? It was very surprising to me, when, listening to the radio recently, I discovered—and later found confirmed in the score—that in the first three movements Beethoven uses almost no minor chords, except in a very small number of cases, when it is impossible, with respect to the natural laws of harmony, to omit minor triads. Even then he uses an escape by leaving many sections in unison, unaccompanied, when the melody is understandable without harmony. Here the intention is clear: in Beethoven's musical vocabulary a minor chord expresses sadness. But he wanted to picture "the awakening of gay feelings on the arrival in the country."

I am ready to forget this hypothesis in favor of a different one, the result of a changed standpoint in regard to evaluation. At the beginning of my career, still under the influence of post-Wagnerianism, I wrote sequences like my contemporaries. This seemed justified to me by the model of all great preceding composers: Bach, Beethoven, Mozart, Wagner and even Brahms, who did not avoid true sequences or slightly varied repetitions. Moreover, since a young composer in this period was intent not only on illustrating the mood and all of its changes, but also on describing every bit of action, a special formulation, the Leitmotiv, seemed obligatory. The Leitmotiv, usually a small phrase, did not consume much space because development, apposition of varied phrases, cadential limitations and other establishing technical requirements, which demanded the space of eight to sixteen measures, became superfluous. A phrase of two measures followed by a sequence ordinarily required a liquidating addition of one or two measures. Thus a little independent segment could be produced which also did not require an elaborate continuation, and was, so to speak, open on all four sides. Properly employed, an esthetic merit is gained by using no more space than the ideas demand, and this is why this technique rather proved a stimulant to the *Neudeutsche Schule*.

It was the Brahmsian school which at this time fought violently against the sequences of the *Neudeutsche Schule*. Their attitude was based on the opposite viewpoint that unvaried repetition is cheap. And, in fact, to many composers sequences were a technique to make short stories long—to make out of four measures eight and out of eight measures sixteen or even thirty-two. It is especially the Russian composers, Rimsky-Korsakoff and Tschaikovsky, who must be blamed for this improper application of an otherwise acceptable technique. And it could have happened that this misuse might have eradicated every higher technical ambition.

Much depends upon the viewpoint whether criteria are judged as merits or as shortcomings. When Schumann speaks of the "heavenly length" of Schubert's music, one might be led to consider length, heavenly or earthly, a merit. But one is disappointed to learn that Hanslick, Wagner's opponent, blames Bruckner for the length of his symphonies. When Brahms demanded that one hand of the pianist play twos or fours while the other played threes, people disliked this and said it made them seasick. But this was probably the start of the polyrhythmic structure of many contemporary scores. There can be no doubt that those who called Mozart's String Quartet in C major the "Dissonance-Quartet" intended merely a characterization, just as they called another quartet the "Drum-

Quartet" and still another the "Hunting-Quartet." It is perhaps no merit to include drums in a string quartet or to describe hunting pleasures. And it does not contribute a thing to their evaluation.

Certainly calling it the "Dissonance" quartet includes a criticism on which an evaluation can be partly based. My own experience proves this. A Viennese society refused the first performance of my String Sextet, *Verklärte Nacht,* because of the "revolutionary" use of one—that is *one* single uncatalogued dissonance.

The expert is in no position to forget what his education has taught him. His code of honor which, for instance, forbids some dissonances, but tolerates others, demands numerous merits as the basis for evaluation. Thus he values a composition more highly only if its themes and melodies are significantly formulated and well organized; if they are interesting enough to hold the attention of a listener; if there is a sufficiently great number of ideas; if they are well connected so as not to offend musical logic; if they are restricted by subdivision to a conceivable size; if monotony is avoided by good contrasts; if all ideas, however contrasting, can be proved to be only variations of the basic idea, thus securing unity; if a thorough elaboration proves that their inner merits surpass their incidental advantages.

Having evaluated the ideas from these viewpoints, the expert might proceed to problems of style: Is the time-space adequate for the importance or the unimportance of the ideas?

Are main ideas distinctly differentiated from subordinate ideas in space by adequate proportions as well as in emphasis, so as always to secure the predominance of the object? Is the breadth of the presentation justified? Is it admissible because of the number of ideas, because of their inescapable consequences, or because of comprehensibility? Is every detail presented in as brief and as condensed a manner as possible?

Does the profundity of the real meaning interfere with the elegance of the presentation and the polish of the surface? Is the material adequate with respect to the medium, and vice-versa? Are heroic themes ascribed to unheroic instruments, such as flute, guitar or mandolin? Is a violin sonata supposed to express passionate emotions adequate for a symphony? Is an instrument as immobile as a contrabassoon required to play a gracious barcarolle? Is musical description stylized tonally and technically to fit the nature of the instruments, as the calls of the nightingale, quail and cuckoo in the *Pastorale Symphony* are suited to the flute, oboe and clarinet respectively? Is the descriptive element incorporated formally and motivally within the basic conditions of the piece? Are states or situations illustrated whose nature is opposed to that of music —as, for instance, expressing repose by slight movement, or silence by sounds, or abstract philosophy by concrete tones? Does the piece elaborate its ideas and material in a technique inappropriate to its style? Are contrapuntal ideas accompanied in a quasi-contrapuntal manner, scarcely producing more than a harmonization? Is the natural phrasing of a homophonic melody confused by the addition of sophisticated counter-melodies, as often happens in popular music? Are dissonances which are not inherent in the tonal content added to simple folk-tunes?

Nor could the expert renounce an examination of the value of the thematic material. He would also have to question the inventiveness of a composer. Was he able to bring forth as much variety as unity and comprehensibility will tolerate and the stimulation of interest demands? Was he able to prove the necessity of the work—that it was forced upon him by an inner urge for creation? Has he been able to produce something which fills a gap in the knowledge and culture of mankind, or, if not that, which at least satisfies a desire for entertainment? In other words, does his product, through novelty, prove to be a desirable contribution? Is this novelty one of essential or subordinate qualities? If derived from essentials, is it of a nature like Beethoven's dramatization of the elaboration, or comparable to the novelty of the structural, emotional and descriptive qualities of Schubert's songs? Or is it like Wagner's entirely new way of building, expressing, harmonizing and orchestrating, thus revolutionizing music in all its aspects?

Has this novelty been produced through a new personality rather than through revolutionary changes, through evolutionary developments rather than through frightening outbursts? Did this novelty come from a personality comparable to a Mendelssohn, a Schumann, a Gounod, a Debussy, etc.,—artists whose ambition was not that of the reformer, though their originality was rich and distinct enough?

Though originality is inseparable from personality, there exists also a kind of originality which does not derive from profound personality. Products of such artists are often distinguished by a unique appearance which resembles true originality. Certainly there was inventiveness at work when the striking changes of some subordinate elements were accomplished for the first time. Subsequently, used consciously, they achieved an aspect of novelty not derived profoundly from basic ideas. This is *mannerism*, not originality. The difference is that mannerism is originality in subordinate matters.

There are many, and even respectable, artists whose success and reputation are based on this minor kind of originality. Unfortunately, the tendency to arouse interest by technical peculiarities, which are simply added to the nothingness of an idea, is now more frequent than it was in former times. The moral air of such products is rather for success and publicity than for enriching mankind's thoughts.

Some values derive from causes or reasons to which influence on creation should not be credited. Creation to an artist should be as natural and inescapable as the growth of apples to an apple tree. Even if it tried to produce apples in response to the demands of a fashion or of the market, it could not. Thus artists who want to "go back to a period," who try to obey the laws of an obsolete esthetic or of a novel one, who enjoy themselves in eclecticism or in the imitation of a style, alienate themselves from nature. The product shows it—no such product survives its time.

There is no essential difference between the criteria of this type of music and the aforementioned. Popular music speaks to the unsophisticated, to people who love the beauty of music but are not inclined to strengthen their minds. But what they like is not triviality or vulgarity or unoriginality, but a more comprehensible way of presentation. People who have not acquired the ability of drawing all the consequences of a problem at once must be treated with respect to their mental capacities; rapid solutions, leaps from assumptions to conclusions would endanger popularity.

This does not mean that in popular music such melodies, rhythms and harmonies as one might expect in higher music must necessarily be excluded. Of course, no such structural problems, no such developments and elaborations as one finds, for example, in Brahms' symphonies, no such contrapuntal combinations like those of Bach can be the object of a popular composer. Nevertheless, listening to popular American music, one is often surprised at what these composers venture with respect to traditional standards. However, for the sake of the popular understanding manifold repetitions, the application of only slight variations and well employed, even if only conventional, connectives are provided.

It seems that friends of popular music have their own code

for the evaluation of what they like or dislike. It is not obvious whether a technical or theoretical knowledge is required; probably instinct serves as judge. Certainly a well-functioning instinct can offer a basis for correct judgment.

But most of the aforementioned criteria for the evaluation of higher music are accessible only to the expert, and many of them only to highly competent experts.

Though there is no doubt that every creator creates only to free himself from the high pressure of the urge to create, and though he thus creates in the first place for his own pleasure, every artist who delivers his works to the general public aims, at least unconsciously, to tell his audiences something of value to them.

Ambition or the desire for money stimulates creation only in the lower ranks of artists. "Money! How can you expect to be paid for something which gives you so much pleasure?"

From the lives of truly great men it can be deduced that the urge for creation responds to an instinctive feeling of living only in order to deliver a message to mankind.

Just as obvious as that music is not created to please, is the fact that music *does* please; that it has an undeniably great appeal to people who "know naught of the tablature"—who do not know the rules of the game.

On the other hand, to depend on the expert—and on those who usurp the role of expert—may prove disastrous. Wagner in his Beckmesser portrayed one such living expert who knew all of the tablature but failed miserably in applying his knowledge to "what doth not with your rules agree." And when Hans Sachs confides more in those who "know nought of the tablature," his confidence is justified.

It is a well known fact that already in the culture of even primordial peoples music's mysterious appeal to men adorns worship of the divinity, to sanctify cultish acts. With primitive peoples it is perhaps even rhythm or sound alone which casts enchantment. But even the culturally high-ranking Greeks ascribed mysterious effects to simple successions of tones, such as expressing virtues and their contrary. The Gregorian Chant does not profit as much from the meaning of the words as does the Protestant chorale; it lives on music alone.

Considering these facts, one might wonder whether the subsequent higher art forms were indispensable for religious ceremony. Whether or not art of a primitive or higher kind enhances the enchanting effect of music, one conclusion seems inescapable: there is a mystery.

My personal feeling is that music conveys a prophetic message revealing a higher form of life towards which mankind evolves. And it is because of this message that music appeals to men of all races and cultures.

Searching for criteria for the evaluation of music, it seems dangerous to ascribe this mysterious influence to all kinds of music regardless of their standard and value. It would be dangerous to admit that one who is a lover of music and sensitive to its charms has acquired the right and capacity to judge its values. How dangerous the consequences of such conclusions can be was recently proved.

The results of the voting for the Metropolitan Opera broadcasts did not include among the six chosen operas a *Fidelio*, a *Magic Flute*, a *Marriage of Figaro*, a *Mastersinger*, an *Eugene Onegin*, a *Fra Diavolo*, a *Barber of Seville*, etc. Democratic as it is, there is one decisive mistake in such voting. Not going so far as to offer only one candidate, political parties would not go so far as to offer forty-six candidates—the number of operas offered. In practical politics the choice of candidates is made by the leaders.

This is perhaps similar to Schopenhauer's demand that the evaluation of works of art can only be based on authority. Unfortunately he does not say who bestows authority nor how one can acquire it; nor whether it will remain uncontested, and what will happen if such an authority makes mistakes. Mistakes like his own, when he, disregarding Beethoven and Mozart, called Bellini's "Norma" the greatest opera.

My accusation of Schopenhauer may be excused by offering myself to the same condemnation: I confess to be guilty of similar crimes. For a long time I had scorned the music of Gustav Mahler before learning to understand and admire it. I once said: "If what Reger writes is counterpoint, then mine is not." I was wrong—*both* were.

On the other hand, in favor of Sibelius and Shostakovitch, I said something which did not require the knowledge of an expert. Every amateur, every music lover could have said: "I feel they have the breath of symphonists."

Experts are also human—but this is not the fault of us composers!

Folkloristic Symphonies [1]

PEACE after the First World War granted political independence to nations which culturally were far from ready for it. Nevertheless even small nations of six to ten million people expected to be regarded as cultural units, nations whose national characteristics expressed themselves in many ways: in their applied arts, weaving, ceramics, painting, singing and playing and, finally, even composing music. Of course, X-Town might have developed individual habits differing considerably from those of Y-Town, from which it was separated by 3,000 feet of mountains. But both demanded general recognition, and attempted to acquire a "place in the sun," seeking the opportunity to sell their national products with profit. The balance of trade was the real idea behind their mock-ideals.

Isolation alone does not guarantee fertility. On the contrary, contact, even with inferiority, can be stimulating. On the other hand, inescapable necessities of life, those emotions of love, mourning, nostalgia, etc., will find individual and perhaps original expression. Whether people live in seclusion or not, they may find their own words, their own tunes, and create their own songs. And if those from X-Town differ no more from those of Y-Town than Dorian differs from Aeolian—there will be enough to be proud of.

If songs of the Southern section of West-Parinoxia show Lydian traits in their otherwise Phrygian texture, dances of the neighboring Northern part of Franimonti may display the opposite: Phrygian influence in Lydian melodies. Such differences constitute individuality to the local connoisseur. There exist such differences, for instance, in the Balkans. Their

1 *Musical America,* February, 1947.

songs and dances are often overwhelmingly deep in expression and attractive in their melodic configuration; they are beautiful and one must love them. The places of origin of these differences, however, are of interest rather to the specialist than to the undiscriminating music-lover.

In spite of high appreciation for these differences, one has to admit that they are negligible in comparison to the differences between folklore and artistic music. They differ perhaps no more than petroleum and olive oil, or ordinary water and holy water, but they mix as poorly as oil and water. Even a Beethoven could apply only a fugato-like, rather simple treatment to a given theme in the Rasumovsky String Quartet, Op. 59, No. 2. And when he marks this theme "Thème Russe" one is inclined to believe that on the one hand it is a homage to his aristocratic Maecenas, but on the other hand an excuse to musical experts, who would understand the obstacles connected with commissions. In order to comprehend this problem it is useful to compare this treatment with that of the scherzo of the Ninth Symphony. Here also a semi-contrapuntal treatment is applied; but the second subject is melodically the continuation of the first. The second subjects to the Thème Russe are only incidental accompaniments without combinatory value. Obviously, this theme is founded on a primitive harmonic progression, which is contrary to the requirements of contrapuntal combinations. Furthermore, in its unpretentious constitution there is no problem which suggests development into a theme.

As a folk dance, the Thème Russe is certainly very pleasant. But that there now exists Russian music is due to the advent of some great composers. Were this not the case, great Irish or Scotch symphonies should have been created, because the folklore of these peoples is of an unsurpassed beauty and full of striking and characteristic traits. On the other hand, some smaller nations whose folk music is not as extraordinary have succeeded in placing in the history of music and into the minds of music lovers representatives such as Smetana,

Grieg, Chopin, Liszt, Dvorak and Sibelius. Characteristically enough, Sibelius contends that his music is not based on national folk music, and I guess that Grieg's also is not. Chopin's rhythms are often derived from Polish dances, but harmonically and in part melodically neither his music nor that of Liszt (or much of Smetana's) differ essentially from Western and Central European styles of their day.

Evidently folklore based on extraordinary or exotic scales displays more characteristics, and perhaps even too many. It seems a nightmare to imagine what might have become of music if Japan had succeeded in conquering America, England and finally Germany. The Japanese idea of music has no resemblance to ours. Their scales are not based on a harmonic concept, or, if so, at least it is not ours. Friends of Eastern Asiatic music claim that this monodic music is capable of such variety as to express every nuance of human feeling. This may be true, but to the Western ear it sounds—ah—different. If it is not completely impossible to add a harmonic accompaniment to melodies of this kind, it is certainly impossible to derive it logically or naturally from these scales. For this reason alone it seems they would rather destroy our music than comply with its conditions.

Even Gypsy music, whose characteristic scales have become influential among several surrounding nations in the Balkans, though it is not as foreign to our ears, has been unable to penetrate the wall separating folk music from art. Whenever Brahms incorporates such a melody in a composition the structure ordinarily will not surpass the implications of a set of waltzes or of a quadrille. In works of higher organization he adds only the flavor, the perfume to his own themes. But he is not forced to enter into foreign territory to express unusual melodic types, as is proved by the last movement of the G Major String Quintet. Liszt's Hungarian Rhapsodies are structurally more profoundly organized than those Romanian Rhapsodies and *Zigeunerweisen*. However, they are chiefly potpourris, forms of a looser construction than what classic masters from Bach to Brahms call "Phantasies."

Much beauty may be credited to natural folklore. No credit is deserved by those "man-made" pseudo-folksongs, whose popularity is acquired through the mass appeal unfortunately exerted by triviality. Silcher, Abt, Nessler and their like in other countries falsified simplicity by substituting sentimentality for artlessness and sentiment—they present only the white-collar man's concept of the man in the street. So also do high-standard composers, who never forget their aristocratic superiority when they descend to their "Im Volkston" songs. They are always at least structurally correct. If one's left leg is too short, one's right leg compensates in that it is too long. But in most of these imitations, there always occur phrases one or more steps too long for which other phrases which are too short cannot compensate. Natural folk music is always perfect, because it stems from improvisation—that is, from a lightning flash of inspiration.

The discrepancy between the requirements of larger forms and the simple construction of folk tunes has never been solved and cannot be solved. A simple idea must not use the language of profundity, or it can never become popular. Everybody will understand the statement that parallel lines are "in all parts equally distant" (Webster). But the scientific formulation that "they meet only at infinity" requires too much thinking and imagination to be generally understood and to become popular.

Genuine folk tunes remain within the narrowest compass of a scale and are based on simple harmonic progressions. Changes of the harmony and figuration of the melody such as, for instance, Bach applies to chorales do not produce new material, contrasts, subordinate themes, etc. Structurally, there never remains in popular tunes an unsolved problem, the consequences of which will show up only later. The segments of which it consists do not need much of a connective; they can be added by juxtaposition, because of the absence of variance in them. There is nothing in them that asks for expansion. The small form holds the contents firmly, constituting thus a small expansion but an independent structure.

A motive, in contrast to this, is incomplete and depends on continuations: explanations, clarifications, conclusions, consequences, etc. The opening motives of Beethoven's Fifth Symphony, Example 1a, can be understood as E flat without the clarifying harmony in measures 5ff, and a melodic continuation by which the third in *a* is transposed in *a'* to complete the C minor triad.

Example 2 shows how the motive of the transition is derived from a reinterpretation of the two main notes E flat and F (marked by *)[2] as tonic and dominant of E flat major, surrounded by B flats.

Example 3 shows how the subordinate theme is related to that and to the first statement of the motive (Example 1a). This is what I call the "method of developing variation."

I cannot remember a single case of deriving subordinate ideas from a folksong by this method. Generally some method is used to make a short story long: numerous repetitions of a short phrase, varied only by transpositions to other degrees, changes of instrumentation, more recently by addition of dissonant harmonies and by what Hollywood arrangers call counterpoints, i. e., "unsolicited gifts" of unrelated voices.

---

[2] See measures 196ff and measures 409-415 in the same movement.

Thus nothing has been said that was not said in the first presentation of the tune.

A composer—a real creator—composes only if he has something to say which has not yet been said and which he feels must be said: a musical message to music-lovers. Under what circumstances can he feel the urge to write something that has already been said, as it has in the case of the static treatment of folksongs?

A real composer does not compose merely one or more themes, but a whole piece. In an apple tree's blossoms, even in the bud, the whole future apple is present in all its details —they have only to mature, to grow, to become the apple, the apple tree, and its power of reproduction. Similarly, a real composer's musical conception, like the physical, is one single act, comprising the totality of the product. The form in its outline, characteristics of tempo, dynamics, moods of the main and subordinate ideas, their relation, derivation, their contrasts and deviations—all these are there at once, though in embryonic state. The ultimate formulation of the melodies, themes, rhythms and many details will subsequently develop through the generating power of the germs.

Put a hundred chicken eggs under an eagle and even she will not be able to hatch an eagle from these eggs.

Defenders of the use of folk tunes as themes for large forms might see an analogy in the utilization of chorales and other folk songs as themes for variations by classic composers. While Bach often derives the voices which contrapuntally accompany the main voice in his chorale preludes from the chorale melody itself, there is no possibility or necessity of a developing growth. One can admit on the other hand that, in primordial specimens, sets of variations serve rather the virtuoso who wants to be brilliant through his technique. In such variations there is seldom any other development than velocity and no other change than the figuration of the instrumental style. The simplicity of the variation is adequate to the simplicity of the folk melody. In the artistically superior compo-

sitions of this kind the "motive of the variation," as I called
it, is derived through "developing variations" of basic features
of the theme and its motive. Thus, in fact, the same compositorial procedure can be observed here as anywhere else in our
established Western music, producing the thematic material
for forms of all sizes: the melodies, main and subordinate
themes, transitions, codettas, elaborations, etc., with all the
necessary contrasts.

A real composer who is accustomed to produce his material
in this logical manner—be it by spontaneous inspiration or by
hard labor—will only occasionally voluntarily renounce starting his composition in his own way, with his own themes.
They will contain many a provocative problem, requiring
treatment. There would not be a larger form, were it not that
this urgency is present, even in the embryonic state, and cannot be escaped. Thus a real composition is not composed but
conceived, and its details need not be added. As a child resembles his parents, so do they correspond entirely to the ini-
tial conception. And they break forth in the same manner in
which the child's first and second teeth break forth, like all
those inconceivable but natural miracles by which creation is
marked.

Real folk music could not exist, or survive, were it not produced similarly: spontaneously, as an inspired improvisation.
It is well known that Franz Schubert liked to improvise
waltzes and other dances when his friends danced. It seems
improbable that real folk music has been composed by pain-
fully adding tones to tones and little segments to little segments. Folk tunes have been improvised singing or playing
by bards, troubadours and other gifted persons. Knowing that
some photographers are capable of forcing better people to
pose in a cheap manner—the left hand on the piano, trying to
find the tones or harmonies which the pencil in the right
hand preserves for eternity—I am always inclined to doubt
whether one like this is a real composer, a real creator.

FOLKLORISTIC SYMPHONIES

It seems that nations which have not yet acquired a place in the sun will have to wait until it pleases the Almighty to plant a musical genius in their midst. As long as this does not occur, music will remain the expression of those nations to whom composing is not merely an attempt to conquer a market, but an emotional necessity of the soul.

Of course, a soul you have to have!

Human Rights [1]

I

IT IS SAD to have to admit that most men consider it their human right to dispute, even to overpower, the human rights of their fellows. Even sadder is the aspect of the world today, which offers no hope of improvement in the foreseeable future.

But this should not stifle our longing for a state of affairs in which the sanctity of each man's human rights is intangibly self-evident. Humanity has been benefited by all such blessings only because an ever-increasing number of people have yearned passionately for redemption until it was granted. All progress in social thinking and feeling which eliminated friction in community life has come about only through the force of such longing.

We must never give up our longing.

Let heathens continue to dispute the immortality of the soul, the faithful must never cease to feel its self-evidence. For even if the heathens were right at present, the force of the longing of the faithful would eventually generate an immortal soul.

And the same thing will happen with human rights, if only we do not stop believing in them—although they are as yet far from being universally recognized or defined.

II

Should the rights of the general law, i. e. the civil law, differ from the human rights, such differences should be designated as follows:

---

[1] Los Angeles, July 21, 1947.

a) Human rights should strive to improve the balance between claims and resistance, even in cases where the civil law has not as yet discovered a solution.

b) A certain minimum of rights unchangeably valid for all peoples and races should be searched for.

The authority to make a declaration of human rights belongs to an organization which views itself as the avantgarde for the development of civil rights.

III

Law is only in the slightest degree an attempt to secure balance. In reality, it is nearly always an expression of power. True, the right of the feeble has enforced recognition up to a point, but it has enforced it in the manner a power enforces its ends. Disagreement arises, if unforeseen consequences had to be accepted because one had been overwhelmed by pity; reaction then is provoked.

IV

The difficulty of establishing right lies in the mutual opposition of those interests which are entitled to protection. Galileo, who cast doubt upon the credibility of the story of Creation, and the Church, which could not permit attacks upon the inviolability of the Scriptures, were equally in need of protection—and equally entitled to it.

In our much-vaunted civilization burning at the stake is out of custom. To a certain degree, at least, one can say what one likes (though let us not forget the "third degree"). After all, Pasteur and Zola had not to suffer physically—but mentally only. And hardly anything (except some annoyance) happened to the doctor who propounded a new theory about diabetes, ten years too early.

War, the father of all things, has again furnished to the world new models, recommended for imitation. Troublesome expressions of all-too-free thinking are eradicated together with their originators. Their books are burned, their authors hanged, full dressed generals without trial; they have no special rights, and feelings of shame are ignored because right is what benefits the German, and only remotely related to human right.

V

Fifty-one percent could hardly be sure of winning a battle against forty-nine percent. But by an election, they gain the ascendancy over a minority, subjugate them, and turn them into slaves.

The claim of protection is acknowledged even if the relation is two percent to ninety-eight percent. But the forty-nine percent minority has lost all its rights—oftentimes even some of its civil rights.

But let us also not forget that microscopic one-man-minority, not more than five to ten of whom are to be found, even in Western civilization, in each century.

VI

A progressive development of civilization and culture, based upon scientific knowledge alone, would eventually have to accomplish equilibrium of conflicting interests. This might not take place for several centuries, for powerful opponents are struggling, and all such interests are recognized. But the more refined the methods of testing rights might become, the more numerous will become the demands. The Archbishop could dare to cuff Mozart without so much as suspecting that thereby he had won his place in the history of music. Who could know, in these days, to what an extent the artist's sense of his own dignity would develop? Who could foresee in these days that a creator might lose lust for life if he faced suddenly a thought contradictory to his dignity?

But, on the other hand, who could foresee that the contumely which was heaped upon the heads of Wagner, Ibsen, Strindberg, Mahler and others by the critics would finally be looked upon as a code of honor? No one could be a really great man without such enemies.

When will human rights—well, not prevent a man from having to undergo such experiences, but at least cause the others to be informed that it is shameful to have occasioned such suffering?

VII

Every scientist, technician, discoverer, poet, painter, or musician who has profited from the acquisitions of one of his predecessors contributes something to the development of his profession—whether this one or that one be an original thinker, or merely one who imitates or utilizes. One must not underestimate the honest craftsman who reworks familiar materials, and one should also not overestimate the original thinker. No one owes everything to himself alone.

Whether or not it must be tolerated that infringement is more highly rewarded than the alien property from which it was borrowed (though never repaid) is after all of subordinate importance. But, often enough, the real originator is taken for the imitator, when the real imitator is a clever propagandist. That is a falsification of the history of the intellectuals—but who cares, except the victim?

VIII

A gold mine, an oil well, a store, a bank, a factory, or even an oil painting cannot be taken away from the remotest descendants of their possessor by anyone. But the protection of owner-rights on intellectual works is restricted by a time limit during which it is a punishable crime to steal from the author or creator, not because such a theft is immoral and dishonorable, but because it would impinge upon the interests of belligerent powers. Because, after this period has lapsed, competition will force the publisher to sell more cheaply, but will still leave him sufficient profit, because he need not pay the author any more. Supposedly the work of art then belongs to the commonwealth, but in reality it belongs to the exploiters. After this period has lapsed, the taking of what is not one's own property ceases to be a punishable crime, though it has not ceased to be a theft. The commonwealth has only that title of possession granted to it by its power. This is senseless not only morally, but also economically; for the interest of the public in the work of art is far too slight to justify its taking upon itself the responsibility of exposing the descendants of the genius to the same misery as the genius himself.

IX

It is tragic that a code of human rights lacks the capacity of defending itself against attacks and annihilation to the same extent as does democracy. Everything which one might undertake in their name would violate the human rights of the attackers—just as everything is undemocratic which might protect democracy.

Their last resort is only persuasion.

X

It looks as if the code of human rights will have to limit itself to a smaller number of claims than its high-sounding title would imply.

XI

Most forms of faith are exclusive, and antagonistic—even militant, challenging, and quarrelsome. It would be self-destruction were they tolerant. Think, for example, of Communistic or Fascistic states, in which faith functions as an instrument of government.

XII

Is it the duty of man to believe in truth? Is the right to believe what is false worthy of protection?

XIII

Surely, the Ten Commandments represent one of the first *déclarations des droits humaines* set forth in word and script. They assure the right to live and to have possessions; they protect marriage, vows, and work, but deny from the very beginning freedom of faith, because there is only ONE God.

HUMAN RIGHTS

XIV

"How can I truly love the good without hating the bad?" asks Strindberg. Consequently, he wants to combat evil—in fact, he *must*. This is why one man has to fight against "bourgeois art," while another must fight against the Palestinian style of architecture because it is qualified foreign to the race, though, however, it stems from the great Adolf Loos.

He who fights will and must conquer, will and must oppress the conquered.

But what are the human rights of those who still believe in defeated art, in defeated ideas?

XV

Music speaks in its own language of purely musical matters —or, perhaps, as most estheticians believe, of matters of feeling and fantasy. One can pass over Richard Strauss' good joke: "I can express in music the moving of a pencil from one place to another." That is not the language in which a musician unconsciously gives himself away, as he does when he formulates ideas which might even frighten him if he did not know that no one can find out what he hides while he says it.

But one day the children's children of our psychologists and psychoanalysts will have deciphered the language of music. Woe, then, to the incautious who thought his innermost secrets carefully hidden and who must now allow tactless men to besmirch his most personal possessions with their own impurities. Woe, then, to Beethoven, Brahms, Schumann and all other "Unknown"[2] composers, when they fall into such hands —these men who used their human right of free speech only in order to conceal their true thoughts!

Is the right to keep silent not worthy of protection?

---

[2] Cf. *The Unknown Brahms*. Under this title an author undertakes to pollute the image of the composer.

XVI

One must also recognize the rights of cannibals. Their claims are based on the instinctive recognition that blood becomes blood, flesh becomes flesh. In view of the primitive devices used to establish this as a scientific fact, one must grant a high rank to such an instinct. It functions more reliably than "tests" on the basis of which suffering humanity is dosed with medicines the deleterious effects of which are already after one year observable.

XVII

Is it human right to be born or is birth control a human right? Is birth control permissible, or is it tolerable to let children decay as if they were surplus? What attitude do religions take?

XVIII

Let us think of the Hindus. They die, millions of them, in a famine, yet it would never occur to them to slaughter a cow, a sacred cow. How can we explain to people of such faith what is the right of men and, in spite of that, expect that they believe in human rights—these men who would die in silence rather than act in a manner contrary to the sanctity of their faith? Compare this attitude to that of the old lady who, when one of her favorite hens was designated for the supper table, first stroked and fondled it tenderly. When she then turned it over to her cook for the necessary preparations, she said, "Poor hen! But you'll taste so good in wine sauce."

XIX

These are real problems, and one could easily become pessimistic about them.

Nevertheless, one must never give up the longing for the universal sanctity of human rights.

In our soul there lies the power of longing with creative intensity.

On Revient Toujours

I REMEMBER with great pleasure a ride in a Viennese fiacre through the renowned Höllenthal. The fiacre went very slowly and we could discuss and admire all the beauty and, even more, the frightening aspects which gave the name to this Valley of the Hell. I always regret that one might never possess nerves calm enough to endure such a slow ride.

At least, when only twenty years later I made a trip by auto through one of the most renowned valleys in Switzerland, I saw almost nothing and my companion on this occasion rather mentioned some of the commercial and industrial aspects this valley offered. In twenty years people had lost the interest to take an eyeful of these beauties and enjoy them.

Of these two cases I had to think, when recently a German —a former pupil and assistant of mine—asked me what he should answer when people demanded from him whether I had abandoned twelve-tone composing, as at present I so often compose tonal music: the Band Variations, Op. 43b, the Second *Kammersymphonie,* the Suite for String Orchestra and several others.

My answer was tuned to the pitch of the two true stories aforementioned, founded upon some historic facts. I said: One should be surprised to find that the classic composers— Haydn, Mozart, Beethoven, Schubert, Mendelssohn, Schumann, Brahms and even Wagner—after Bach's contrapuntal climax, in spite of their in essence homophonic style, so often interpolate strict counterpoint, differing from Bach's counterpoint only by such features as the progress in music had brought about; that is, a more elaborated development through variations of the motive.

One cannot deny that the combination of these two structural methods is surprising; because they are contradictory. In contrapuntal style the theme is practically unchangeable and all the necessary contrasts are produced by the addition of one or more voices. Homophony produces all its contrasts by developing variation. But these great masters possessed such an eminent sense of the ethical and esthetical requirements of their art that the problem whether this is wrong can simply be disregarded.

I had not foreseen that my explanation of this stylistic deviation might also explain my own deviations. I used to say: The classic masters, educated in admiration of the works of great masters of counterpoint, from Palestrina to Bach, must have been tempted to return often to the art of their predecessors, which they considered superior to their own. Such is the modesty of people who could venture to act haughtily; they appreciate achievements of others, though they themselves are not devoid of pride. Only a man who himself deserves respect is capable of paying respect to another man. Only one who knows merits can recognize the merits of other men. Such feelings might have developed in a longing once again to try to achieve, in the older style, what they were sure they could achieve in their own more advanced style.

It is a feeling similar to that which would give preference over the fast automobile, to the slow, leisurely fiacre; which desires occasionally to dwell in the old, rather primitive living circumstances of our predecessors. It is not that we wanted to nullify all progress, though machinery has eliminated so many crafts: bookbinding, cabinet making, calligraphy, wood-carving and—almost—painting.

When I had finished my first *Kammersymphonie,* Op. 9, I told my friends: "Now I have established my style. I know now how I have to compose."

But my next work showed a great deviation from this style; it was a first step toward my present style. My destiny had forced me in this direction—I was not destined to continue in the manner of *Transfigured Night* or *Gurrelieder* or even *Pelléas and Mélisande*. The Supreme Commander had ordered me on a harder road.

But a longing to return to the older style was always vigorous in me; and from time to time I had to yield to that urge.

This is how and why I sometimes write tonal music. To me stylistic differences of this nature are not of special importance. I do not know which of my compositions are better; I like them all, because I liked them when I wrote them.

The Blessing of the Dressing

PROFESSIONALISM in music had made great progress in the nineteenth century. But in the last quarter of this century there were great numbers of amateurs still alive—amateurs of all grades, ranging from violin players who could only play in the first position to those who could compete with excellent concert virtuosi. Many people had their weekly chamber music in their homes. They played all kinds of combinations: piano duets, violin and cello sonatas, piano trios and even string quartets. And also professional musicians played in string quartets or other combinations solely for their love of music, without aiming at another profit than this pleasure. I myself have participated very frequently in such groups and my profit from this work was a rather comprehensive acquaintance with classical chamber music.

The abolition of amateurism stems from the ambition of amateurs who wanted to compete with the professionals. The result was extremely destructive to the art of music. The necessities of competition now forced rivals to use improper means in order to make a success, and what is even worse is that those who as amateurs had formerly been impartial and unselfish, and ready to support needy or unfortunate artists, promoters of the arts, were now in the market themselves. Instead of buying music, instead of attending concerts, instead of enjoying music, they themselves demanded support.

While the rank of an artist, of a performer, of a virtuoso could still easily and speedily be determined, it became more difficult and demanded more time to do the same when a multitude of composers, of newly made-up geniuses began to appear on the horizon. Some of them had learned the craft thoroughly and at least knew something; others had been instructed superficially and used their commonplace talents to compete successfully with hard-working, serious composers.

To this increase in the number of musicians who composed corresponded proportionally an increase of those who taught composing. And to the lowering of the standard of the composers corresponded that of the standard of their teachers. However, one must state that there were many who had themselves been instructed competently and who were able to communicate their own knowledge; there were also composers of talent and experience, some of whom might have engaged themselves in research of the past or even the present, finding solutions to problems, describing compositorial techniques and improving teaching methods; there were also specialists who could not or did not want to teach more than a limited field of theory—for instance, harmony only, or counterpoint, or both, but not compositorial techniques. Unfortunately the great majority helped through their own incompetence to increase the number of ignoramuses who knew only a few tricks.

On the average, teaching was not bad. Really harmful was the condition that these teachers were professionals and had to make their living teaching. Accordingly, they had to accommodate to the pressure of competition and this meant "teaching individually"—that is, making it easier for those who had less talent, without making it difficult enough for the talented.

It was not true, as it is in sports, that you had to accomplish something surpassing the average. A teacher who wanted to have a sufficient number of well-paying pupils had to reduce his demands on talent, skill and industry. Did the talent not suffice for symphonies or operas, a pupil could write songs or short piano pieces and finally even only popular music. Always a private teacher had to lead his pupils to a certain success.

I must admit that I never made such accommodations. When I said in my *Harmonielehre* that I taught individually, it was not to spare my pupils the effort to do the best. I would change nothing else but the order of the course, but did not omit matters a musician must know. You could postpone some problems which were too difficult in the beginning for later. You could give exercises preliminary to the harder task. But I had never given in with my main demands.

There existed also students who did not intend writing serious music. They only planned to write popular music—operettas and the like. Many of them were sincere enough to admit their own limitations and conceded their restricted aims.

I once had a pupil who had started harmony with me. About two months later he stopped taking lessons. He had been offered a position as second music critic on a great newspaper and was afraid too much knowledge might have unfavorable influence upon the spontaneity of his judgment. He made a career as a critic and even as a pedagogue.

As a teacher I never taught only what I knew, but rather what the pupil needed. Thus I have never taught a student "a style," that is, the technical peculiarities of a specific composer, degraded to tricks, which to the master in question might have been the solution of a torturing problem. And if I say in the preface to my *Harmonielehre* that I tried to invent something for every student to serve his personal necessities, that does not mean that I made it easier for one of them.

Especially not, because I was insisting on one main demand: that a composer must not compose two or eight or sixteen measures today and again tomorrow and so on until the work seemed to be finished, but should conceive a composition as a totality, in one single act of inspiration. Intoxicated by his idea, he should write down as much as he could, not caring for little details. They could be added, or carried out later.

I used to say that the composer must be able to look very far ahead in the future of his music. It seems to me this is the masculine way of thinking: thinking at once of the whole future, of the whole destiny of the idea, and preparing beforehand for every possible detail. This is the manner in which a man builds his house, organizes his affairs, and prepares for his wars. The other manner is the feminine manner, which takes into account with good understanding the nearest consequences of a problem, but misses preparing for the more remote events. This is the way of the dressmaker, who might use the most valuable material without thinking whether it will last long, if only it makes the desired effect now—right now. It need not last longer than the fashion will last. It is the manner of some cooks who prepare a salad without questioning whether every ingredient is the right thing and fits well with every other, whether they will mix satisfactorily. There will be a French dressing—or perhaps a French-Russian dressing—put on top of it, and this will connect everything. Composing then, in harmony with such advice, is a matter of producing a certain style.

I consider it as one of my merits that I did not encourage composing. I rather treated most of the hundreds of pupils in a manner that showed them I did not think too much of their creative ability.

I do not mean to say that I made it intentionally difficult for my pupils—rather, that I had no control over it. This can be proved by the following fact.

For many years I had tried in vain to teach my pupils some discoveries I had made in the field of multiple counterpoint. I worked hard to formulate this advice in a manner conceivable for a pupil, but I did not succeed. Only once, in one of the best classes I ever had, I considered the presentation of this problem and its solution as final, and I asked the class to compose for the next lesson something applying the methods emerging from my solution.

It was one of my greatest disappointments. Only one of my students had tried to use my advice, and he had misunderstood me as much as the rest of the class.

This experience taught me a lesson: secret science is not what an alchemist would have refused to teach you; it is a science which cannot be taught at all. It is inborn or it is not there.

This is also the reason why Thomas Mann's Adrian Leverkühn does not know the essentials of composing with twelve tones. All he knows has been told him by Mr. Adorno, who knows only the little I was able to tell my pupils. The real facts will probably remain secret science until there is one who inherits it by virtue of an unsolicited gift.

The harshness of my requirements is also the reason why, of the hundreds of my pupils, only a few have become composers: Webern, Berg, Eisler, Rankl, Zillig, Gerhart, Skalkottas, Hannenheim, Strang, Weiss. At least I have heard only of these.

One more effect derived from it: all my pupils differ from one another extremely and though perhaps the majority compose twelve-tone music, one could not speak of a school. They all had to find their way alone, for themselves. And that is exactly what they did; everyone has his own manner of obeying rules derived from the treatment of twelve tones.

While I was not able to teach my students a style—I admit I was not able to do it, even if I would have overcome my dislike of so doing—there are other teachers who can do this and only this.

Thus we see a great number of composers of various countries and nationalities who compose about the same kind of music—music, at least, of such a similarity that it would be difficult to distinguish them from one another, quite aside from the question of their nationality. Advice for composing is delivered in the manner in which a cook would deliver recipes. You cannot fail; the recipe is perfectly dependable. The result is: nobody fails. One makes it as well as all the others.

Astonishingly, each considers it his national style, though different nationalities write the same.

It is the true internationalism of music in our time.

This is my Fault

IN THE PREFACE to *Pierrot Lunaire* I had demanded that performers ought not to add illustrations and moods of their own derived from the text. In the epoch after the First World War, it was customary for composers to surpass me radically, even if they did not like my music. Thus when I had asked not to add external expression and illustration, they understood that expression and illustration were out, and that there should be no relation whatsoever to the text. There were now composed songs, ballets, operas and oratorios in which the achievement of the composer consisted in a strict aversion against all that his text presented.

What nonsense!

What is the purpose of adding music to a text?

In the ballet, music should hide the noise of the steps.

In radio it is a substitute for a curtain, when the writers of murder stories are not capable of marking a change of the scenery otherwise. They still could use a bell.

In the movies, besides also serving as a curtain, it is supposed to underscore moods and actions.

But songs, operas and oratorios would not exist if music were not added to heighten the expression of their text.

Besides, how do you make sure that your music does not express something—or more: that it does not express something provoked by the text?

You cannot prevent your fingerprints from expressing you. But your handwriting unveils very much to the graphologist.

I remember how Busoni was the first to claim that music in opera must not express what is expressed by the action.

The opera is principally the product of four factors: the text, the music, the stage and the singer. If one of these constituents is allowed to disregard what the others do, why should they not also enjoy the same privilege? For instance, the singer?

Could not Monostatos ask Sarastro to dance a "pas de deux" with Pamina? Or could not Lohengrin immediately after his arrival sell the swan to a butcher and start auctioning his gondola? Or would King Mark not better sing his "Dies, Tristan, mir?" (This, Tristan, to me?) as if he were surprised over a beautiful Christmas present offered by Tristan?

The greatest incongruity with what the text expresses is its contrary. Why not play a pianissimo song to the ride of the Valkyries? Why not play a boogie-woogie when Wotan walks across a rainbow in Valhalla? This at least would make sure that you did not fail and that your music might fit quite well to another opera, but not to your own.

I will gladly admit that your tonal and modal products are as expressionless as a poker-face—but why are you trying your bluffs on music?

In the near future there will be machines like the lie-detector, and the craft of the graphologists will be developed and supported by similar devices and gadgets. They will accurately reveal what you hide and tell what you expressed—your bluff will then be called.

To the Wharfs

EVERYBODY in town had relatives on one of the four boats. Everybody, whether he was fearing for the life of a relative, a friend, or only a member of the little community—everybody was waiting with great apprehension for news of the fate of the boats, now missing for ten days. Other boats, smaller and larger ones, which had escaped the terrific storm, sailors and passengers they had picked up, reported about the great tragedy of the ocean that had cost the lives of so great a number of people and had caused enormous losses to ship owners and insurance companies.

Hope had almost entirely vanished. Only a few people still believed in the safe return of their relatives. All prayed in churches for the unfortunate victims of the sea.

It was late in the afternoon, the sun already half down, when an elderly man, running down Main Street, cried in French with all his power:

"The boats, I see them, they are coming home!"

In a few seconds the streets were crowded with people, all running in one direction, to the ports, to the wharfs. They all cried aloud in French: "Aux quais! Les vaisseaux sont retournés. Ils se trouvent aux quais!" Or in English: "To the wharfs! The boats are returning. They are already at the wharfs—aux quais!"—O. K.

Index

INDEX

[223]